Curing Mad Truths

CATHOLIC IDEAS FOR A SECULAR WORLD

O. Carter Snead, *series editor*

The purpose of this interdisciplinary series is to feature authors from around the world who will expand the influence of Catholic thought on the most important conversations in academia and the public square. The series is "Catholic" in the sense that the books will emphasize and engage the enduring themes of human dignity and flourishing, the common good, truth, beauty, justice, and freedom in ways that reflect and deepen principles affirmed by the Catholic Church for millennia. It is not limited to Catholic authors or even works that explicitly take Catholic principles as a point of departure. Its books are intended to demonstrate the diversity and enhance the relevance of these enduring themes and principles in numerous subjects, ranging from the arts and humanities to the sciences.

RÉMI BRAGUE

Curing Mad Truths

Medieval Wisdom for the Modern Age

University of Notre Dame Press

Notre Dame, Indiana

University of Notre Dame Press
Notre Dame, Indiana 46556
www.undpress.nd.edu
All Rights Reserved

Copyright © 2019 Rémi Brague

Published in the United States of America

Library of Congress Cataloging-in-Publication Data

Names: Brague, Rémi, 1947- author.
Title: Curing mad truths : medieval wisdom for the modern age / Rémi Brague.
Description: Notre Dame, Indiana : University of Notre Dame Press, [2019] |
Series: Catholic ideas for a secular world |
Includes bibliographical references and index. |
Identifiers: LCCN 2019011964 (print) | LCCN 2019014704 (ebook) |
ISBN 9780268105723 (pdf) | ISBN 9780268105716 (epub) |
ISBN 9780268105693 (hardback : alk. paper)
Subjects: LCSH: Theological anthropology—Christianity. | Humanity. |
Civilization, Medieval. | Philosophy, Medieval.
Classification: LCC BT701.3 (ebook) | LCC BT701.3.B73   2019 (print) |
DDC 190—dc23
LC record available at https://lccn.loc.gov/2019011964

∞ *This book is printed on acid-free paper.*

CONTENTS

ACKNOWLEDGMENTS

Material in this book has been featured in a variety of prior publications or presented as lectures that are heretofore unpublished:

Introduction. Unpublished.

Ch. 1. Deneke Lecture given in Lady Margaret Hall, Oxford University, Oxford, UK, February 25, 2011, reprinted from *The Modern Turn*, edited by M. Rohlf (Washington, DC: Catholic University of America Press, 2017), 291–305.

Ch. 2. Lecture given at New York University, New York, November 1, 2014, previously published in German in *Internationale Katholische Zeitschrift Communio* 41 (2012): 279–88; in French in *Revue Catholique Internationale Communio* 37 (2012): 95–105.

Ch. 3. Lecture given at New York University, New York, November 1, 2014, and at the Lumen Christi Institute, Chicago, November 5, 2014; summary in *The European Conservative* 12 (Summer/Fall 2015): 39–42.

Ch. 4. Lecture given in Boston on October 11, 2015, first published in *Proceedings of the American Catholic Philosophical Association* 89 (2015): 35–43.

Ch. 5. Lecture given at the University of Notre Dame, November 19, 2015; unpublished.

Ch. 6. First Lorenzo Albacete Lecture, given at the Crossroads Institute, New York, October 22, 2016, in *Cooperatores Veritatis:*

Scritti in onore del Papa emerito Benedetto XVI per il 90° compleanno, edited by Pierluca Azzaro and Federico Lombardi (Vatican City: Libreria editrice vaticana, 2017), 297–317.

Ch. 7.   Speech given at the congress of the ALLEA [European Federation of Academies of Sciences and Humanities], Vienna, April 18, 2016; unpublished.

Ch. 8.   Lecture given at the IESE Business School, Barcelona, October 16, 2009, and at Brigham Young University, Provo, UT, October, 21, 2011; unpublished.

Ch. 9.   Lecture given at the congress of the Vanenburg Society [now called the Center for European Renewal], Dubrovnik, Croatia, July 3, 2014; at the Lumen Christi Institute, Chicago, October 14, 2014; and at the Catholic University of America, Washington, DC, November 19, 2014; unpublished.

Introduction

The many-faceted English novelist, essayist, and wit G. K. Chesterton (d. 1936) characterized the world we are living in, namely "the modern world," with a phrase that became famous, not to say hackneyed, in some circles. According to him, the modern world is "full of the old Christian virtues gone mad."[1] Let me take my bearings from this characterization.

This quip is often misquoted under a generalized form as dealing not with "virtues" but with "ideas" or "truths." The formula is not to be taken without caution, however, for the authentic wording turns out to need correcting, whereas the latter, more general form, is, in the last analysis, the deeper and truer one. Chesterton gives the cause of the going-mad of the virtues immediately afterward: "They have gone mad because they have been isolated from each other and are wandering alone." But he doesn't tell us what madness is—the reason being that he gave us a very sensible answer a little earlier in the same book: "The madman is the man who has lost everything except his reason."[2] The modern world plumes itself with its being utterly rational. It might be the case that it has painted itself into the same corner as the poor fellow that Chesterton described. Not by extolling reason, but by doing that against other dimensions of human experience, thereby depriving it of the context that makes it meaningful. More on that later on.

Now, I should like to ask a question: Does it make sense to speak of "Christian virtues," virtues that we can responsibly call by the adjective "Christian," that is, virtues that are supposed to be specifically Christian and not to be found elsewhere? I would answer, No.

Twenty years later, Chesterton implicitly qualified his overhasty phrase and penned a far more felicitous formula:

> The fact is this: that the modern world, with its modern movement, is living on Catholic capital. It is using, and using up, the *truths* that remain to it out of the old treasury of Christendom; including of course many *truths* known to pagan antiquity but crystallised in Christendom. But it is *not* really starting new enthusiasms of its own. The novelty is a matter of names and labels, like modern advertisement; in almost every other way the novelty is merely negative. It is not starting fresh things that it can really carry on far into the future. On the contrary, it is picking up old things that it cannot carry on at all. For these are the two marks of modern moral ideals. First, that they were borrowed or snatched out of ancient or medieval hands. Second, that they wither very quickly in modern hands.[3]

According to Chesterton, and in the wake of earlier authors such as A. J. Balfour or Charles Péguy, the modern world is basically parasitic, preying on premodern ideas.[4] One will pay attention to the important rider according to which the medieval heritage included "of course many truths known to pagan antiquity but crystallised in Christendom." The lackadaisical "of course" is far from being evident or, at least, from being commonly admitted, for many people insist on the radical break between the "pagan" and the Christian eras. The shift from the ancient world and worldview to what followed it, a period usually called the "Middle Ages," can be painted in different shades, including the modern representation of a clean slate enabling a new departure from scratch.

Be that as it may, the basic thesis still holds good—namely, that the modern world doesn't leave the capital it is living on unscathed, but corrupts it. For it gives each of the elements it borrows from the earlier worlds a particular twist in order to make it subservient to its own aims.

Three Ideas Gone Mad

Let me now give some examples of premodern ideas that were taken up by modern thought but made to run amuck. Three of them quickly sprang to my mind, but there may be some more:

(a) The idea of creation by a rational God underlies the assumption that the material universe can be understood by human beings. But modern thought does away with the reference to a Creator and severs the link between the reason supposedly present in the things and the reason that governs or at least should govern our doings. This tearing asunder the fabric of rationality produces what I would call, if I were allowed to indulge in punning, a low-cost *logos*. It fosters a renewal of a kind of Gnostic sensibility. We are strangers in this world; our reason is not the same as the reason that pervades the material universe. Human reason should have as its main goal the preservation of its concrete basis in human life. Hence, it should assume that the existence of mankind is a good thing, that its coming-into-being through the intermediary agency of evolutionary processes, from Darwin's "warm little pond" or even from the Big Bang up to now, has to be condoned.

(b) The idea of providence was received by modern thought but "secularized" and warped.[5] The man in the Clapham omnibus keeps believing in progress and, although he has to admit its failures, gets surprised and indignant when things go awry. We more or less believe that we can do what we like, follow just any whim, and mankind will find a way to escape the dire long-term consequences of the policies we follow. We let the coming generation bungee-jump, and we hope that somebody will fasten the elastic or give them a parachute to put on while they are falling. We don't beget children, but we expect the stork to bring us grandchildren so that they can clean up our ecological mess and, not to forget, pay for our retirement.

(c) The idea of requiring mercy for one's faults and begging for pardon was kept, and is even rampant in our European countries. We still live in a "guilt-culture" (Ruth Benedict). It even looks like we are witnessing a weird comeback of the great flagellant processions that took place during the Black Death, the difference being that we prefer to flog our ancestors rather than ourselves. In any case, repentance is separated from the hope of being forgiven. We thereby get some sort of perverse sacrament of

confession without absolution. To be sure, acknowledging one's short-comings or even crimes and asking for forgiveness is a noble and necessary behavior. But it verges on the pathological when there is no authority to pronounce the liberating words of absolution.

The Project

The modern world plays the ideas that it corrupts in a particular key, which I have tried elsewhere to describe as being the project of modernity, or rather modernity *as a project*, in contradistinction to what I have called a *task*.[6] A project is what we decide to undertake, whereas a task is entrusted to us by some higher power: nature in pagan style, or God in biblical style.

Suppose, now, that the modern world has its underpinnings in a project that is in the long run doomed to failure. The reason is that it lacks legitimacy: the whole point of this enterprise, since Francis Bacon's clarion call, is to bring to human beings many extremely good things, like health, knowledge, freedom, peace, plenty. This is very much to its credit, and far be it from me to dream of jettisoning achievements that are undoubtedly blessings, even if reality keeps falling short of many expectations. But there is a snag: the modern worldview can't furnish us with a rational explanation of why it is good that there should be human beings to enjoy those good things.[7] The culture that flatters itself with the sovereignty of sober reason can't find reasons for its own continuation. If this is the case, if the modern world can't ensure its perpetuation, will all the goods that were willy-nilly embarked on be engulfed in its shipwreck? And, in particular, what becomes of the virtues or ideas—or rather truths—that it has driven to madness? My thesis is that they are to be salvaged from the straitjacket, released from the loony bin, and given back their sanity and dignity—a dignity which is premodern in nature, that is, rooted in the ancient-cum-medieval worldview.

Back to the Middle Ages?

Elsewhere, I have put forward the rather provocative thesis that what we need is a new Middle Ages.[8] What I mean thereby is certainly not the utterly negative image of the alleged "Dark Ages," for this image is itself the result of the propaganda war waged by the modern project in search of its own legitimacy and fighting for it against a straw man.[9] The medieval period, such as historical research enables us better to know it, was an age in which richness and misery, innovation and conservation, enlighten-ment and obfuscation, happiness and wretchedness were inextricably mixed. By the way, this is a feature that it shared with each and every pe-riod which we know of in the course of history, including the one which we have to live in at present. Medieval people were exactly as smart and as stupid, as benighted and as enlightened, as generous and as wicked, and so on, as we are now. But they were not so in the same way. When modern times set on, they brought about "new learning and new igno-rance"[10] in a perfect balance. Some new things were learned while other ones were forgotten, either not paid attention or even given good rid-dance to.

The trouble was aptly captured by the age-old fable of the two bags we carry, the one on the chest, the other one on the back.[11] We find it easy to see the stupidity of other, earlier people rather clearly, whereas our own possible shortcomings, which are unknown to us, might very well make us the laughingstock of later generations. Therefore, I won't en-deavor to show what is commonly called the "actuality" of medieval ideas. Trying to show that something is still or again "actual" consists, more often than not, in pointing out that some of its aspects resemble what is commonly held to be true in the present time, or even contain a foretaste of it. Now, this suggests that the ultimate criterion of truth, or at least of interest, is whether an idea tallies with our own opinion. We would thereby betray an utterly self-centered outlook. What I wish is, to the contrary, that we should get some distance from our own worldview. For my claim is that our own modern outlook is seriously flawed, so that it would hopelessly distort whatever would be found to fit into it. I would rather radically turn the tables and plead on behalf of some sort of return to some sort of Middle Ages. I cautiously say "some sort" twice in order to avoid misunderstandings and caricatures.

I don't mean to advertise for one of those "backward to . . ." (German, *zurück zu* . . .) that have been giving German intellectual life its peculiar rhythm since the idea of going back to Kant (*zurück zu Kant*) was launched by the philosopher Otto Liebmann in his *Kant und die Epigonen* of 1865. Many features of the medieval worldview are simply obsolete—

features, by the way, that had been inherited from previous philosophers and/or scientists like Aristotle, Ptolemy, or Galen and shared with all medieval thinkers in all religions. They are obsolete because they were simply wrong.

Furthermore, I contend that we won't have to decide whether we want a return to some sort of medieval outlook or not. This is not a matter of taste and of choice, but a necessity, if enlightened mankind is to resist its temptation to suicide and survive in the long run. One way or another, our culture will have to make a step backward to *some* Middle Ages. As a consequence, I won't endeavor to show that we *should* get back to premodern ideas, let alone to preach in favor of such a move. I won't need to do that. Whether we will have to get back to something medieval or not is in fact Hobson's choice, for we will have to, no matter what.

The question pending with such a retrocession is this: To what kind of Middle Ages shall we be forced to fall back? To a barbarian kind, whose cruelty and stupidity would beat even the dark image we sometimes have of it? Or to a humane, civilized kind? Needless to say, if I had to cast my ballot, I'd vote for the second kind. And my hunch is that we should begin right now to bolster our dropping zone with the utmost care if we don't want to undergo an age the horrors of which would dwarf both the alleged darkness of the remote past and the too real monstrosities of the twentieth century.

Such is the intention of the present work: salvaging the virtues, ideas, or truths that the modern project has driven to insanity by retrieving the premodern form of those good things. What drives me to launch into such an endeavor is not an antiquarian taste for the past, let alone a nostalgic or reactionary cast of mind. Let the dead bury their dead. Instead of preparing this necessary return out of nostalgia for the past, quite on the contrary, I do it because I surmise that the premodern form of some basic ideas might prove more stable than their modern perversion, hence more fraught with future, more capable of nurturing our hope.

Plan

In order to pave the way for my enterprise of rescuing premodern ideas, I will first have to show again that the modern project is a failure, for the basic reason that I have just sketched.[12] This is the aim of chapter 1. It takes up a passage from a bulkier work of mine.[13]

Chapter 2 elaborates in more detail the contradictions of the atheistic worldview that is the nerve of the modern project. The chapter lays bare that worldview's capitulation before the irrationality of the instincts, whereby reason gives up its own claim to sovereignty in an act of high treason.

Where a recovery of old verities is at stake, the hoary concept of the good, common to the Platonic tradition and to the first account of creation in Genesis, must play the lead. Without that concept, humankind can't go on existing both as a biological species and as endowed with an opening on rationality (ch. 3).

As for the ideas, virtues, or truths that I plan to redeem from their modern state of humiliation, I must first exhibit their genealogy, especially in the case of those intellectual goods that are commonly thought to be modern inventions or to have had to wait for modern times to meet with the conditions of their fulfillment. I will show that we should get a clearer consciousness of their nobility by unearthing their roots in the very origins of Western culture, and not only in "Athens" but in "Jerusalem" as well: both nature (ch. 4) and freedom (ch. 5) are rooted in the Hebrew Bible. To be sure, concepts are there not as such, in the form of concepts, for those tools were minted in the forge of Greek philosophy only. Nevertheless, the biblical outlook casts them in a narrative form.

Culture is a basic—and even the basic—dimension of the human. It did not have to wait for the biblical revelation for it to thrive. But it underwent a decisive turn when the latter came to its fulfillment with Christianity. Culture was demoted from the sovereignty that it was and still is tempted to claim for itself. But at the same time, it received a place and a value of its own. It doesn't consist only in humankind spontaneously shaping itself in order to cater to its own comfort; culture is rather an endeavor to answer the call and challenge of what is anterior and superior to human beings (ch. 6).

The modern idea of "value" arises from the attempt to find the origin of whatever is good in human subjectivity and, deeper still, in life's self-assertion. Values replace ancient, "pagan" virtues as well as biblical commandments. Now, virtues will have to stand their ground against "values," which they can do if and only if they are the way in which the human answer to the basic divine commandment "Be!" takes a concrete figure (ch. 7).

Human association itself, the so-called society, will have to take into account the family as the place in which nature and culture mingle and interact, so that continuity and innovation can further each other (ch. 8).

Civilization itself as the highest goal of mankind on this earth, as the flourishing of whatever is human and deserves this name, will prove to rest on the *logos*, on the kind of articulate speech which makes rationality possible in the first place and which has been defining the human being since the Greek philosophers. This *logos* itself supposes that meaning and intelligibility are somehow present in the world, and hence that we are somehow at home in it (ch. 9).

CHAPTER ONE

The Failure of the Modern Project

To begin with, I will argue in favor of the rather strong thesis that the modern project failed. In my opinion, it is high time we had the pluck to acknowledge this failure and looked for the behavior that could enable us to cope with the situation that arises from it. The failure of such a project presupposes first that there was, or still is, such a thing as a modern project. As a consequence, I will first have to describe it. By examining the very idea of a project we can understand what the modern project is driving at.

Modern Times as a Project

I am far from being the first to speak of the "project of the modern age," the "modern project," and other, similar phrases. I'm afraid I would be at a loss to tell who first coined the phrase "the modern project." Anyway, it was launched in philosophical circles thirty-five years ago by Jürgen Habermas in a lecture that he gave in 1980 and that was widely echoed. The theme was "enlightenment as an unfulfilled project." This was part of the strategy of the German philosopher who sides with this project and looks forward to fulfilling it or at least to fostering it.[1]

The observation that the Enlightenment remained a project that never was totally fulfilled is to be found not only as the provocative battle cry of a philosopher but as the sober result of research in the field of the history of ideas. This is the case in the United States with Louis Dupré, in France with Pierre Manent.[2] Yet, whereas the phrase crystallized only recently, Europe did not have to wait very long to become the stage of a strange phenomenon which, interestingly, took place precisely at the threshold of the age that we call "modern." Europe witnessed the rise, at strategic places, of words that designate the attempt, the experiment, the project. It is enough to name Montaigne with his *Essais* (1580), from which Bacon, and in his wake so many others, took up the title.[3] As for the stress on experimentation, it is all the more conspicuous that the intention to experiment is earlier than its real implementation. Bacon's alleged experiments are for the most part mere fantasy. Even real scientists never were more talkative about the necessity of experimenting than when the facts on which they pretended to ground their hypotheses were mere thought experiments.[4] Galileo even lets the cat out of the bag in his *Dialogues on the Two Main World Systems* (1632), when he proudly confesses that he never tried to conduct an experiment, since he is fully confident that the result would necessarily come out as he expected.[5] Experimenting is more than a scientific ploy; it is a whole atmosphere. Nietzsche makes a far-reaching observation when he writes that what characterizes the nineteenth century is not the triumph of science but the triumph of method over sciences. The same author called his time "the age of attempts" (*Zeitalter der Versuche*).[6]

Furthermore, the fact that modernity as a whole is a project has been not only felt but reflected upon for a long time. When Descartes wanted to start what was to become the *Discourse on Method*, he initially called it "the project of a universal science that could lift our nature up to its highest degree of perfection."[7] Sixty years later, in one of the earliest of his many works, Daniel Defoe, who had still to wait for more than twenty years to become the famous author of *Robinson Crusoe*, wrote *An Essay upon Projects*. He begins by pointing out that projects are fashionable, so that it would not be amiss to call the epoch "The Projecting Age." He thinks first and foremost of the speculations on great overseas trade, such as the one that had ruined him some years earlier. For overseas trade furnishes us with a privileged paradigm, because it is, says Defoe, "in its beginning, all project, contrivance, and invention."[8]

In 1726, Jonathan Swift caricatures the members of the Royal Society under the features of the absent-minded passengers of the flying island of Laputa, to whom he gives the name "projectors." He ascribes to them ludicrous inventions.[9] He thereby creates the type of the absent-minded professor whose numerous popular incarnations are famous, like the savant Cosinus or Professor Nimbus—two heroes of French comic strips. Yet the word "projector" has nothing derogatory or ironic in itself. People can claim it as an adequate means to define their doings. It is to be found in Joseph Glanvill's tract of 1668 advertising for the Royal Society; and in Mary Shelley's novel, Frankenstein chooses it to designate himself.[10]

Late modern philosophical anthropology stressed the notion of project as defining the peculiar status of man among, and in contradistinction to, other beings. Sartre enlarged its use in an anthropological context and shifted it from "having" to "being." According to him, the project is part of the very definition of man, who is "nothing short of his project."[11] Let us stop awhile and look at Sartre's formula: "I am my own project."[12] It was and is still touted by the whole Western intelligentsia, who repeatedly wield it as a weapon whenever one attempts to invoke something like identity and tradition. The utterance makes sense as long as it remains a bombastic version of the platitude that we are not bound to carry on doing what was done up to now by our forebears. Yet, taken literally, the formula doesn't have a leg to stand on. For what makes it the case that the project is *mine*, that it is *my* project? If I am myself the result of a project, this project can't be mine.

We will see later on that the idea of a project shifted from the active to the passive, from the project launched by man to man being the project of some unknown, and in any case unnamed, agent. The history of ideas brings to the fore, and thereby confirms, the inner dialectics of concepts.[13]

The Word "Project"

The word "project" in itself has no shortage of meanings. Its Latin form does not correspond to any word in the Roman vocabulary. To be sure, ancient Latin was familiar with the adjective *projectus*, which means "jutting"; used as an image, it more often than not has a derogatory undertone, for instance when someone speaks of an excessive ambition.[14]

But the substantive is not attested in antiquity. A pro-ject is first of all, most obviously, what the etymology of the word suggests—that is, a throwing (*jacere*), a motion in which the mobile body (missile) loses contact with the mover and forges ahead. This is the very phenomenon that ancient physics failed to account for, or that it could pigeonhole into its framework only through far-fetched theories that had little convincing force for intuition, like the so-called *antiperistasis*. Strangely, modernity, which can be and was considered as the age of the pro-ject, was at the same time the period in which physics began by making sense of throwing *tout court*, thereby introducing concepts that were to lead to the Newtonian idea of inertia.[15]

Choosing to describe an activity in the key of the project implies in any case a break between the subject and the object of the projecting. Furthermore, this choice implies a necessary forgetting of the subject, who, precisely because he rests on himself, can hardly take himself as the object of his own reflection and must leave in the shade whatever is not his project. That this project is his own, that it stems from himself, that it expresses himself, including dimensions that remain hidden to himself— such are the elements that the subject must ignore if he only wants to be able to act.

As a consequence, one can elicit the three basic ideas of modernity as project from the mother image of a throwing. For a project implies a new interpretation of the three dimensions of time: (1) toward the past it implies the idea of a new beginning, of a beginning from scratch, so that whatever came before will be forgotten; (2) toward the present, the idea of a self-determination of the acting subject; (3) toward the future, the idea of an environment that will yield further opportunities for action and that pledges that that further action will be rewarded with achievement ("progress").

Who Is the Projector?

The question is, Who projects? According to the premodern—that is, ancient and medieval—worldview, there was something like a project of man's life. Yet it was not man's project, but the intention of a higher power, Nature or God, something like Providence.

The oldest example of the idea, and of the word, may be the ancient Egyptian *sḥr*. The word is interesting in itself, since it is the causative form ("to let somebody do something") of the verb *ḥr*, which means "to fall."[16] It is to be read in the famous Story of Sinuhe, which hails from the Twelfth Dynasty (about 1800 BC). The main character had to flee Egypt, for reasons that remain shrouded in mystery, and to spend a part of his life outside of the Nile valley, which amounted for an Egyptian to an exile, not to say a damnation. Yet it turns out that this fact, a bad thing in itself, had positive consequences. The story has a happy end: Sinuhe is called back by the king, returns to Egypt, and is sure to be buried there. Reflecting on his flight, he says, at least according to the most likely translation: "It was like the project of a god" (*yw my sḥr ntr*)—although other translators have the more humdrum "as though it might be a god."[17]

Be that as it may, the idea of providence does not designate something posited in man's hands, but something higher. The Stoic *pronoia* has as its subject a nature that is not distinguished from the godly nature—or we may say the same thing in the other way, a god that is not distinguished from the eternal living Fire that creates everything out of itself and periodically brings it back to its origin.

Biblical and Christian providence has as its subject a personal and loving God who cares for his creatures. Christians do not conceive of God's providence and man's prudence as excluding each other. On the contrary, they take rather seriously the deep linguistic identity between the two words, which both stem from the same Latin one.[18] Classical thinkers of the Christian, Latin West like Augustine and Aquinas conceive prudence as being given by God to man, in the same way as providence endows each and every creature with the tools that enable it freely to reach its own goal—that is, the good that its own nature is striving for.

Providence and project are the two poles that could roughly define the difference between the premodern and the modern outlook.

Project and Task

Now, there is a question that I left unanswered up to this point. This is quite an obvious one, and I am sure that my readers must be fidgeting: What is the *content* of the modern project? I have been harping on the idea that modern times are a project, but I never said what exactly they project to do. I hold that the content is already there in the very idea of a project. The project is its own content.

There are many works by historians and philosophers, some outstanding, which shed light on some aspects of the modern project. I drew heavily on their work, but I need not name them here. Whenever we follow those historians and philosophers and try to describe the content of the modern project, we get a host of features, like autonomy of mankind, becoming adult, getting emancipated from the bonds of external powers, hence a policy made able to rule itself without having to take its bearings from cosmology or theology. In some extreme versions, we will even get the intention of turning upside down the relationship of man with whatever is before and above him (the natural and the divine)—such a relationship as obtained throughout premodern times. Relying on nature becomes mastering nature. Depending on the divine as one's measure becomes defining one's own yardsticks—"creating values," and in some cases doing away with God. Yet all those aspects can be summarized in the idea of a project. This is all the more the case if we pay attention to the following fact: it is in no way necessary for human endeavors to understand themselves as being a project. I suggest that we look at a genus that we could call "enterprise" and divide it into two species. One of those two species is the "project." But alongside it there is another species that I suggest we call "task."

The task possesses properties that oppose the three characteristics of the project that I have just highlighted. Every aspect changes signs: in a task, (a) I am entrusted to do something by an origin on which I have no hold, and which I don't always even know and must look for; (b) since I have received from elsewhere what I have to do, I must ask myself whether I am equal to my task, agreeing thereby to be dispossessed of what was, all the same, irrevocably entrusted to me; and (c) I am the only one responsible for what I am asked to fulfill, and I can't possibly off-load it onto another who could pledge for the success of my action.

It has been repeatedly pointed out that the whole gear of images and slogans that undergird modernity is biblical in origin: we inherited from the book of Genesis the idea of a domination of nature (1:28), and from Saint Paul the metaphor of reaching adulthood, doing away with tutelage, and by so doing, emancipating ourselves (Gal. 3:25; 4:2–4). This requires qualification, by the way, especially in the case of the first claim.[19] Anyway, observations of this kind may either legitimize modernity or, on the contrary, compromise the Bible, on which we foist responsibility for the darker sides of modernity.

Now, with this concept of a task, we may be in possession of the criterion that enables us to tell apart modernity and the biblical heritage. For all the biblical images that are commonly called to our mind in this context, including the idea of a straining forward (*epekteinomai*) in Paul's epistles of the captivity (e.g., Phil. 3:13), must be understood in the key of task rather than in the key of project.

Making Experiments

Let me now introduce a second basic idea of modernity, which follows from the first. Wherever the idea of a project plays the lead, the very figure of Truth changes. Truth becomes the result of an experiment.

I already alluded to experimenting when mentioning the strange fashion of the vocabulary of "project," "attempt," "essay," and so on in early modern times.[20] Now, the idea of experiment originated and spread in the ambit of natural science. But it took a metaphysical turn in German idealism, and first of all with Kant, who reflects on the method favored by Bacon.[21] It began to be some sort of confirmation of the idealistic postulate with the young Schelling. In 1799, Schelling interprets the philosophy of Fichte, to which he still adheres, by taking up the metaphor used by Bacon, and later by Kant, according to which every experiment is a question put to nature, which she is compelled to answer. But he adds: "Every question contains a hidden judgment a priori; every experiment that really is an experiment is a prophecy; the very practice of experimentation [*das Experimentieren selbst*] is a production of phenomena."[22]

So the idea of experimentation went beyond its original realm, which is the one in which it has a rigorous meaning—that is, the natural sciences—and invaded the whole domain of life at large. For instance, and to begin with, in the realm of politics: according to the authors of the Federalist Papers, the young American republic is an "experiment."[23]

Ernest Renan, in a work written in 1848, but published in his last years, gets near to the idea of life as an experiment and gives as an example Saint-Simon, the utopian: "What would happen if we could add to scientific experimentation the practical experimentation of life?"[24] Some ten years later, in Britain, John Stuart Mill's liberal ethics (1859) encourages what he calls "experiments of living."[25] The idea of experimentation shifts thereby from theory to practice. This is the case in Nietzsche: philosophical effort is a series of attempts "to reach a form of life that we haven't yet reached."[26] It finds a cancerous, and even caricatural growth, in the realm of aesthetics.[27] And still more, maybe, in the thirst for originality and eccentricity at all costs in the realm of everyday life.

Being an Experiment

A wholly different situation obtains when man is no longer considered as the subject, the experimenter, but rather as the object about which an experiment is mounted. It is supposed that the very existence of man is nothing more than an attempt made by some impersonal power. The idea is not devoid of roots in the ancient world. A rather unclear verse in the book of Job asks: "Isn't there for man a service [*tsâvâ*] on earth?" (7:1a, my trans.).[28] The Septuagint translated this as "Is not the life of man on earth a trial [*peiratērion*]?" And Augustine, who followed the ancient Latin translation, had "tentatio est vita humana super terram" (The life of man on this earth is a test).[29] Maimonides interpreted the biblical story of Abraham's temptation (*nissayôn*) as a trial through which man's obedience toward God becomes manifest not to God himself, who knows everything, but to man, which thereby becomes conscious of his own abilities.[30]

Yet all this remains embedded in the representation of a God who, albeit mysterious, is believed to be good and to do good. And it has to be, for the very idea of enterprise, trial, endeavor, attempt, and so on implies that a failure is not excluded. If the experiment is a task, we may hope that it will be successful because it was entrusted to us by a benevolent power. But if it is a project, there is no other warrant than a vague belief in "progress." Therefore, a sea change occurs when the subject that carries out the experiment takes the impersonal aspect of Nature as an indifferent force, such as she is conceived of by moderns. An intermediate stage is represented by Villiers de l'Isle-Adam's novel *L'Ève Future* (1886). The fictional Thomas Edison, on the verge of creating an artificial woman, reminds his sponsor: "Both of us are part of the experiment."[31] The attempt still has human beings as agents, but they are drawn into their own experiment and carried further than they expected.

A further step is taken when man is conceived as being the merely passive object of an experiment whose subject is nature. The idea appears, to the best of my knowledge, for the first time in Goethe. A friend of his reported a conversation held in the poet's garden in summer 1809: "Let us think of Nature as if She were sitting in front of a gaming-table and unceasingly shouting: 'Double!' That is, as if She luckily, nay infinitely played with what She had already won through all the realms of her action. Stone, animal, plant, everything is again put at stake after some lucky throws of that kind, and who knows whether Man in his whole is not merely a throw towards a higher goal [*ein Wurf nach einem höhern Ziele*]?"[32] Goethe said this fifty years exactly before Darwin's path-breaking masterpiece, *The Origin of Species*, but some forerunners of the idea of evolution already had adumbrated such ideas.

A whole tradition in anthropology conceives of man as being not a fully achieved being but a sketch of sorts. I already quoted Sartre's words to the effect that man is his own project.[33] But here, on the contrary, man is the object of a project that he doesn't control. Fichte writes: "All the animals are perfected and ready; man is only sketched and projected" (*angedeutet und entworfen*). Heidegger defines the life of what he calls *Dasein* as a "project" (*Entwurf*), and later on deepens the idea by making of the project not a whim or initiative of man any longer, but a fundamental feature of Being.[34] Mankind as a whole is an experiment of life. The idea is to be found in a poem that Rainer Maria Rilke wrote in Muzot on June 4, 1924, and that Heidegger put at the center of his interpretation of the poet: we are a risk (*Wagnis*).[35] The song of the poet is echoed by the cold prose of the British biologist Julian Huxley: "[Humanity] is an experiment of the universe in rational self-consciousness. . . . The only significance we can see attaching to man's place in nature is that he is willy-nilly engaged in a gigantic evolutionary experiment by which life may attain to new levels of achievement and experience."[36] Finally, it is found at a very recent date in Hans Jonas's *Das Prinzip Verantwortung*

(The principle responsibility), although the whole point of his book is advocating prudence in the face of any utopian technological adventure. He mentions the "ontological experiment [*Versuch*] that Being launched with Man."[37]

The Dialectics of Experimentation

Let us ponder awhile the implicit logic of the idea. If man is the result of a dice throw, and if the agency that produced him (God, Nature, Being, or what not) can wager another throw, this means that the throw that resulted in the creation of man is not Nature's last word. Hence, the result of that throw, man, is, in comparison with what might come after him, a relative failure. In the words of Nietzsche's Zarathustra: man is to the Overman who is to come what monkeys are to human beings.[38]

The dialectics are the same as the ones that underlie the idea of progress. It was brought out very soon, even in the Middle Ages, for instance in the discussion between the Persian physician and freethinker Muhammad ibn Zakariyya al-Rāzi and his contemporary the Ismaili propagandist Abu Hātim al-Rāzi.[39] If a continuous progress obtains, the present is, to be sure, supposed to be better than the past. What is now future will be past, but the present will glide into the past earlier than the future. But, since the present is doomed to become the past of a better future, it is at the same time demoted to being nothing more than a preliminary stepping-stone.

Little wonder that the idea according to which man is an experiment was followed, some decades afterward, by another, less pleasant idea: man is a *failed attempt*. I have not yet been able to spot its first use with any certainty, but it became a hackneyed theme from the second half of the nineteenth century, probably because it was in keeping with the general Darwinian and Schopenhauerian atmosphere of this period.

The idea of man as a failure occurs even in the private correspondence—though the general tone is urbane banter—of a Franco-Austrian diplomat with a smattering of Kant and Schopenhauer, Alexander von Villers. He writes in a letter of 1873: "I hold Man for a failed experiment [*misslungener Versuch*] of nature that she is about to give up."[40] The idea hardly left Western consciousness. The German sculptor and playwright Ernst Barlach (d. 1938) is quoted to have said: "Man is a failed attempt [*fehlgeschlagener Versuch*] of nature."[41]

This failure could take on a very concrete dimension. The empowerment of man, man taking his destiny in his own hands, was what the modern project was all about. Now, this sovereignty of man over himself very well could turn out to be the possibility for man definitely to put a stop to the experiment. The failure itself would thereby be entrusted to man. He would draw the negative conclusion and ratify the experiment's own condemnation by committing suicide.

Three years after Villers—that is, in 1876—in his *Diary of a Writer*, the Russian novelist Dostoyevsky imagines a "materialist" committing suicide out of sheer boredom. He is supposed to have asked in his farewell letter the following question: "What if Man was put on earth only for some sort of reckless experiment [*проба*; proba], only in order to see whether a being made like him would succeed in living on earth or not?" The saddest thing is that "there isn't anybody who attempted the experiment, there is nobody whom we could curse, everything happened simply according to the inert laws of nature."[42] The same author discreetly puts forth an analogous idea four years later, in the famous legend of the Grand Inquisitor, told by Ivan, one of the Brethren Karamazov. Dostoyevsky has his Grand Inquisitor characterize human beings as "unfinished, experimental [*пробные*; probnye] beings, created for derision."[43]

Risk

Modernity, thus, conceives of human history as an experiment. Yet there are not many people who recognize the consequence of this passage of human things under the yoke of the experimental—namely this utterly simple fact that, if a laboratory experiment can have a conclusive result, it can have a negative one, too. In other words: an attempt can fail. How is it that so few realize so simple a fact? It is as if a trace of a secularized faith in Providence remained and fed confidence in experimentation.

Let me here quote the British scientist James Bernal: mankind, by increasing its own wisdom, by knowing more and wanting more, will risk more, and by so doing will risk its own destruction. But "this hardihood, this experimentation, is in fact the essential quality of life."[44] Bernal, who was a Marxist and even a staunch supporter of Stalin and of Lysenko's bogus genetics, is thereby taking sides—strange bedfellows—with Nietzsche, who makes "attempt" (*Versuch*) into the very figure of Truth.[45]

Nietzsche is among the few—perhaps he is even the only one—who considered the possibility of an irretrievable failure and honestly acknowledged it. Be that as it may, he has his Zarathustra say, in a passage that remained unpublished: "We are making an experiment [*Versuch*] with Truth! Perhaps mankind will thereby founder! Never mind, go ahead [*wohlan*]!"[46] This is quite a brash formula. We might sober up and ask: What if, in fact, the experiment yields a negative result? What if mankind invents contrivances and/or adopts modes of behavior that endanger its own survival in the long run? The trouble is that, if the experiment does fail, so that mankind as a whole walks the plank, one may ask: who will have another try?

The modern project brought about the possibility of its own demise. It looked for an autonomous mankind. It wanted mankind to be set on its own ground, to be determined by itself and by itself only. Modernity, at least in its late form—say, from the forties of the nineteenth century onward—endeavored to give up any external, transcendent reference point. This is, by the way, the period in which the word "humanism" and its cognates were coined and given their present-day shade of meaning, first in Germany, then in Britain and in France.

Suppose mankind can determine itself, by itself and only by itself: Why should it choose *to be* rather than *not to be*? Why should self-determination receive a positive interpretation? What reason could tip the scales in favor of being rather than not being? Since we can't create ourselves, the choice is between accepting ourselves—hopefully while trying to improve ourselves—and destroying ourselves. And self-destruction is somewhat easier than self-acceptance and/or self-improvement.

The Unanswered Question

This is not an academic question any longer. That mankind did endanger and keep endangering its very survival is nowadays a matter of common knowledge. It has even been putting it in jeopardy for quite some time.

Let me quickly bring to our minds the main dangers. Two are obvious and trite: atomic warfare and the destruction of the biological environment. I would add a third one, less glaring: the low birthrates that could lead to a general shipwreck of mankind, beginning with the most "modern" countries. Many strategies are proposed for us to obviate some of these challenges, and some are implemented. I need not belabor what has become obvious: the media are full of that.

On the other hand, a question is not answered, and not even asked in proper terms: Why should there be human beings? To quote one of the deepest British thinkers, Bertie Wooster: "Well, who wants to keep the human race going?"[47] The "intellectually negligible" young gentleman unexpectedly echoes the question asked by a character in Tolstoy: "For what purpose should it perpetuate itself, the human genus?"[48] In a nutshell: Why is the existence of human beings better than their non-existence or disappearance? I mean, to be sure, their peaceful extinction. A violent disappearance is out of court. We can find obvious moral objections against inflicting suffering and death on our fellow human beings. We can further level the same kind of objections against poisoning the earth and spoiling the life of other people. But how can we say that not having children is per se morally wrong? In the first two cases, we obviously harm other living beings. But whom do we harm by not having children? It might even be the case that begetting them is morally wrong. This is at least the thesis defended by a South African philosopher by the name of David Benatar.[49]

The endeavor to ground the humanity of man on man himself was successful as far as promoting a decent behavior among people was concerned. Earlier types of mankind looked for a ground of social life and organization either in something suprahuman—Nature or God—or in a mixture of both, in a divinized Nature or in a God hardly distinguished from his creation. We do not need such a thing for us to organize our being-together, at least in principle. We must only negotiate how we will get along with each other on the basis of our interests. To be sure, this will happen provided we are clever enough to understand where our real interest lies and to take into account the long run. Yet, I repeat: at least in principle, for us to build a decent society, we need, to quote a famous, albeit imaginary utterance of Alexander Hamilton, "no foreign aid." But a society, decent or not, has first to exist, and it is made of human beings. Now, to repeat: why should there be human beings?

What does the failure of modernity consist of? Modernity can't answer the question about the legitimacy of mankind unless it gives up its own project. The title of the present chapter, "The Failure of the Modern Project," almost boils down to a tautology. Modernity failed because it understood itself as a project. If we stick to this project, we are at a loss about how to explain that mankind as a whole has to be. In order to do that, we need some fulcrum, we need Archimedes's *pou stan* (where to stand). In other words, on the one hand we can produce, and we do produce, a great many good things. I don't mean only material goods. Heaven forbid that I should indulge in one more version of the reactionary critique of consumerism, of so-called materialism, and so on. I am not that sweet on such discourse, especially when it is voiced by well-fed people. Modernity can produce and does produce higher goods that are social and cultural in nature: the possibility for large masses to live decently under the rule of law, to have access to education, museums, to mention only a few examples. Which is very much to its credit, and we must be thankful for that. On the other hand, the modern project is unable to tell us why it is good that there are people to enjoy those goods. To give an answer, we need to shift to a higher, metaphysical, gear.

CHAPTER TWO

Atheism at the End of the Tether

Another way for me to make my point about the failure of the modern project is the following thesis: atheism has failed, hence it is doomed to disappear in the long run. Our task consists in bringing this fact to consciousness and drawing the consequences that it brings about. When so doing in a lecture, I often get the impression from my listeners that I am belaboring the obvious. Now, the problem is that the majority of our contemporaries are unwilling to face either this fact or its consequences. We even live among various attempts at camouflaging it. Let me unmask them.

Victory of Atheism?

Against my thesis, we are tempted to shrug our shoulders, since the contrary seems to be the case. Would it not be more accurate to speak of a triumphal march of atheism? This is the way in which many atheists see the situation. Many polls show that the number of church attenders is plummeting, at least in Europe, that is, in countries that bear the stamp of Christianity. My own country, France, which used to proudly claim to be the "eldest daughter of the church," has been since the Enlightenment and the 1789 Revolution the spearhead of secularization in formerly Catholic countries.

To be sure, religions today are enjoying an unexpected comeback, especially in their most radical forms, for example in the most spectacular—because violent—way in Islam, but in Hinduism as well and, more surprisingly, in Burmese Buddhism, as recent events have shown. Growth is taking place also in a more peaceful guise, in groups such as the Haredim in Judaism or among so-called evangelicals in Protestant Christianity.

The answer of atheists is ready: all these are rear-guard battles, doomed to be short lived. Believers are all the fiercer because they somehow feel that time is working against them. The progress of science and of technology that is narrowly linked up with it brings about, irresistibly, a secularization of life. The steamroller is on the move. We only have to be patient. Secular Europe is the avant-garde; the rest of the world will follow suit.

What lends this hope some grade of plausibility is the fact that, on the level of society, atheism carries the day. In *Thoughts on French Affairs*, which he wrote as soon as December 1791, Edmund Burke made the point that atheists have given up their traditional bashfulness and shifted to a more outspoken, and even more provocative, attitude: "Boldness formerly was not the character of Atheists as such. . . . But of late they are grown active, designing, turbulent and seditious."[1] Today, he would express himself more forcefully. Among the leading minds of late modernity, there were many atheists, who advertised for their unbelief and attacked religion. The names of Marx, Nietzsche, and Freud are in all memories.

Today, we have to do with people whose intellectual quality is not a match against the thinkers whom I have just mentioned. But they are noisier and receive in the mass media a larger echo.

The Successes of a Nontheistic Worldview

Furthermore, spectacular achievements are very much to the credit of atheism. Let me mention two examples, one from the theoretical, one from the practical realm. Both are impressive in their depth and width.

First, on the theoretical level, modern physical science, "written in mathematical language,"[2] succeeded in putting forward a very accurate and fruitful description of reality. This description has no need of the "God hypothesis," to allude to the well-known dialogue between the French astronomer Laplace and the emperor Napoleon. The personal piety of many scientists doesn't play any role in this matter. When they do physics, they work without reference to God. They feel no need to use him as a "stopgap" (*Lückenbüsser*).[3] By this token, one needs no religion—or no more religion—when one looks for an "explanation" of the world.

Second, on the practical level, modern political thought and practice succeeded in showing that societies can organize themselves without a suprahuman principle of legitimacy. As early as 1682, the French philosopher Pierre Bayle took up the hoary question, already asked and answered by Plutarch, as to which is worse, atheism or superstition,[4] and transposed it to the social and political level, defending his famous paradox according to which atheism is not more dangerous for the state than superstition, and even that a society of atheists would be more docile than one of religious enthusiasts.[5] One century afterward, our societies began to make of this intuition or wager a concrete reality, each in its own style, from the American "wall of separation" to the untranslatable French *laïcité* and so on.

Be that as it may, on balance, we may conclude that, in order to orient ourselves in the material world and in social organization, we need no religion. Therefore, some sort of atheism is possible. But which sort? And can this position be held in the long run?

As for the first question, let me make two observations on this kind of atheism. First, it is not necessarily militant, as an aggressive conviction trying to do away with any belief in God. It exists first and foremost as the methodological principle that the Divine must be put into brackets. The word "agnosticism" was coined exactly for this purpose, by the English natural scientist and indefatigable advocate ("bulldog") of Darwin's doctrine of evolution, Thomas Huxley. In Victorian England, outspoken atheism was hardly the thing. Therefore, in the course of a discussion held in 1869 at the Metaphysical Society, Huxley suggested that his own position should be called another, less offensive name, namely "agnosticism."[6] Second, agnosticism is not a stance that concerns religious questions only. The same modesty and soberness are to be found when what is at stake is our knowledge of physical phenomena. The positivism of Auguste Comte and of Claude Bernard makes a basic principle of the renunciation of insight into the ultimate causes. Scientific inquiry should content itself with expressing, in the most precise way, with the help of mathematical language, the relations that obtain between observable phenomena. Why what is is what it is, why it is how it is, are questions that science is not allowed to ask, let alone to answer.[7]

A Sickness unto Death

As for the second question, my thesis is that, in the teeth of all its successes, atheism, even in its milder form of agnosticism, contains a lethal drawback, a "sickness unto death."

For there is a question on which atheism hasn't a bare word to tell us. What is more, it grounds itself on the decision to give up any possibility of answering it. This fundamental question is, If we admit that there is on this earth a being, known as *Homo sapiens*, that is able to give an account of the universe that surrounds him and to live peacefully with his fellow human beings, in both cases without having to look up toward any transcendent reality—would it be good that such a being should exist and keep existing?

To put it otherwise: We can sketch a merely immanent description of physical reality that enables human beings to conquer the world and to exploit it for their own advantage. We need not uncover the ultimate truth about reality, as long as the description we make of it "works." We can set rules for the living-together of human beings in a merely immanent way. It is enough for us to conceive of an implicit or explicit compact through which human beings lay on themselves the duty to spare each other, because it is in their interest to do so. The ultimate goal of the mastery of nature through technology and of the social organization through politics is that mankind should go on existing, and even improve its lot, not only by getting more and more commodities and comfort but by building a more and more satisfactory social situation. Now, the question whether such an existence and/or progress is something we should wish and foster has remained unanswered, and not even been asked. For this question, atheism has no answer, and can't have any. Therefore, it doesn't even want to have any. In order to substantiate this claim, I must venture some words on the self-defeating character of atheism.

Dialectic of Atheism

The failure of atheism is a direct consequence of its success. By this token, we may be allowed to speak of a "dialectics," with the same meaning as in the well-known "Dialectics of Enlightenment" of Adorno and Horkheimer.[8] Yet, whereas the masters of the Frankfurt School remained on the level of ideas, we have to do here with a dialectics that could take utterly concrete features. Let me briefly outline this dialectic.

The project of modern atheism consisted in emancipating man. Man was to decide on his own destiny, he had to give his own law to himself, which we somehow loosely call "autonomy." In former times, this was not the case. This was not even possible, if we have to trust the way in which the modern project tells its own story. Man had to set his life according to principles that lay outside of him. The overarching principle was in some cases the beautiful order of the cosmos (a phrase that boils down to a tautology), which man had to imitate. It was in other cases a divine law which man had to go by.[9] The two points of reference are intertwined: the God who issues the commands is at the same time the God who gave the world its order: the Legislator is the same as the Creator.

Now, modern times refuse more and more decidedly to look in those two directions. Their ideal would be to let man rest on a human basis only, so that any reference to an Outside, to an Other, to a Higher would be excluded, or even become meaningless. To put it as the young Karl Marx did, punning on the word "radical" and its Latin etymology: the root of man is man himself.[10] The nineteenth century minted a name for this ideal, and that name is to be read in the young Karl Marx, too: "humanism." This humanism, precisely because it does not admit any higher authority than man, is unable to pass judgment on man's value or lack of it as such. Man can't possibly speak either in favor of himself or against himself. As a matter of course, it is very likely that man would take a positive view of the existence of man. But such a biased acquittal would be utterly worthless.

In a lecture he gave right after the Second World War, Jean-Paul Sartre brought this out by poking fun at an utterance of the poet Jean Cocteau. The multifaceted French painter and writer tells us about a character seated in an aircraft that is flying above some mountain chain. He admires the landscape, and still more the inventive mind of man, so that he exclaims: "Man is terrific." This may be true, but, Sartre asks, Who is speaking? Certainly neither a dog nor a horse, hence not an unbiased umpire, but—a man. Now, it is clear that nobody can judge himself objectively.[11]

The Concrete Form of Self-Destruction

The question I asked above—that is, Is this good, that there should be human beings?—might be whisked away as merely academic. It *would* be academic if two new elements had not been on the stage for some decades. The first is that man at present possesses the possibility of doing away with himself. The question about suicide has existed since the earliest times. It received a theoretical treatment in Greek philosophy, especially in the Stoic school. This dealt with the individual who had to face exceptional circumstances. What is new is that the problem has taken a collective dimension. The human species is now able to commit an all-encompassing suicide. It possesses the means that could bring this about. Let me mention here three:

(1) Since the beginning of industrialization, man has been spoiling the environment. This could lead to a situation in which the existence of man would become impossible.
(2) Since the discovery of atomic energy and of its possible military use, mankind has possessed the faculty to wipe itself out in a moment, through an all-out nuclear war.
(3) With chemical contraception, each generation can freely decide whether there will be a next one or none at all. This third possibility of extinction would be peaceful, piecemeal, hence hardly visible.

In a long footnote to his *La Profession de foi du vicaire savoyard* (Profession of faith of the Savoyard curate) Jean-Jacques Rousseau took up the comparison that already had become hackneyed in Bayle's time but had taken a new turn, since modern authors had replaced "superstition" as the adversary of atheism with "fanaticism."[12] He rounds it up with a pithy formula: the principles of atheism "don't cause the death of people, but they prevent them from being born."[13] We may observe that atheistic regimes of the twentieth century produced mass murders on a far larger scale than religious wars ever did—what Rousseau was fortunate not to know. But let us suppose, for the sake of argument, that his formula is true. Rousseau goes on: to be sure, fanaticism lets blood flow; but it prompts people to great enterprises—a rather strange idea. On the other hand, atheism, even if it does not kill anybody, reveals itself as being more lethal in the long run.

So much for the first of the two newly appearing elements that changed the terms of the problem. With the second one, we take a step further: annihilation, which already had shifted from merely logical possibility to real possibility, becomes a temptation, because of a second fact. This second fact is that man calls in doubt his own legitimacy. We can look at this once again from three points of view:

(1) Man is no longer convinced that he has the right to conquer and exploit the earth.
(2) Man is no longer convinced of his superiority over against the other living beings. He might be the worst of all predators.
(3) Man is not even sure that he distinguishes himself from other living beings by radically different features. There is no quality leap between human beings and, say, higher apes.

The Enlightenment Project Endangered

As a matter of course, we very well could content ourselves to imagine that the survival instinct will look after man and ensure his existence. This may have been the case in former times. It was thought highly probable that man as a species would carry on existing because people would keep reproducing themselves. But Schopenhauer tried to show that sexual instinct is hardly more than a trap through which the will to live fools us without giving a damn about the happiness of individuals.[14] Can we answer him?

The trouble is that the appeal to instinct would do away with the whole project of Enlightenment. I don't mean thereby only the movement that became conscious of itself and chose this name in eighteenth-century Europe, but the project of philosophy in the whole breadth of its achievements. This project is as old as Socrates and his endeavor to assign a task to every professional person, to compel him to show his competence, which such a person was to do by explaining why exactly he does what he does, by "giving an account," in Greek *logon didonai*. This generally meant that every action without exception should be, in principle, justified by reasons. Now, are we allowed to give up the quest for a ground when what is at stake is the very being of mankind? If we did that, we would have to face something unbearable: we would entrust to unreason the existence of the only being who can be the carrier of reason. We meet here a paradox that was already pointed out on another level: natural science represents a fantastic triumph of reason, but at the same time it claims to show that reason is merely a product—and an unintentional product, an epiphenomenon—of evolution, that is, of a movement that was led by blind and irrational forces.

Yet, though the first paradox is bad enough, with the second one, we would be in a still worse predicament. If reason stems from unreason, we can hardly reproach her for that. But in the case which I am dealing with now, if reason freely surrendered to unreason, it would arguably amount to committing suicide and high treason.

Most concretely, we hear everywhere that the best way to hamper the population explosion that some people still fear is education, and especially school for girls. This may be true. But what is in any case above any doubt is that such a method is morally far superior to compulsory measures like sterilization. Furthermore, it is possible, and even highly probable, that it works better, too. Yet we can deduce from this observation a rather unpleasant consequence: the more intelligent, the more learned is a human group, the more barren it must be. Or conversely: the more stupid and ignorant, the more fruitful. This unpleasantness was felt already in the nineteenth century by no less than Darwin in person.[15] Present-day European demography furnishes us with an almost experimental proof of this equation. It is probably not by chance that the decrease in birthrates affects Europe, and there the educated bourgeoisie, and in the rest of the world the countries and social classes that are supposed to be the most "progressive."

Cause and Ground

Now, mind you: I am not claiming that the shrinking of religious faith in Europe or elsewhere could be the *cause* of the lower birthrates. Looking for causes is already in itself a dubious endeavor. Historians are always reluctant to do that. But admittedly one does, one must, take one's bearing from the fact that such causes, most probably, are a tangled skein of factors that influence each other. In order to see more clearly in this maze, one could and should mobilize sociology, psychology, economics, and so on, all fields in which I have no competence.

I would like here to draw upon a very old, very classic distinction, the one between cause and ground. A fact has causes; an action has grounds. A cause explains what is the case already; a ground concerns what we can bring about in the future. If one could discover the causes of an action, this action wouldn't be free any longer, it wouldn't be an action any longer, but rather a mechanism.

Finally, where the lower birthrates among educated people come from and where they lead is a matter of indifference. To be sure, researching why some individuals or even couples resolutely insist on remaining childless is a fascinating object for sociologists and psychologists.[16] Nevertheless, what we desperately need here is not an explanation, but a reason for us to act. We absolutely must be able to tell *why* the existence of human beings on this earth is a good thing.

If the project of Enlightenment is to be successful, man needs a ground for man to go on existing, and to exist as man in the full meaning of "man," as a rational and free being, not only as a biped without feathers. Man needs a point of reference that can legitimate his existence on the earth—which doesn't mean that it legitimates each of his whims, and certainly not the ruthless exploitation of the planet. The existence of a suprahuman instance that can affirm the existence of the human species is the first content of religion. This instance is, to quote Aquinas's famous formula, *quod omnes nominant Deum* (the one whom all call God).[17]

Now to be quite concrete and matter-of-fact: we need a category of human beings who can bring together in harmony faith and reason. We need it not in order to make human life more beautiful, not as an oil of sorts that could make social life easier, but in order to ensure the continuation of the human adventure. The question is no longer whether we can do without God, but with what kind of God we shall have to live, if we want mankind to live on. The God of the Bible and of the Christians is not the only possible one. There are, besides him, the God of other religions, the God or gods of neo-pagan or para-pagan movements, and into the bargain the God whom Pascal called "the God of the philosophers and of the scientists." My personal hunch is that the God of the Bible and of the Christians could be a very good candidate.[18] But this is another story.

Answer to the Objections

Now, as in a scholastic *quaestio disputata*, we have to answer the arguments that plead to the contrary, the *videtur quod non*.

As for science chasing religion as a better explanation of the world: it is already dubious to understand religion in general as an explanation of physical phenomena. In order to give an account of those phenomena, there is little doubt that the scientific worldview is far more efficient. But one is allowed to ask whether any religion ever intended to do that. The study of the worldview of the so-called primitive peoples shows that they hardly care about the structure of the world, let alone about its causes or the way it came into existence.[19] In later religions, one could quote utterances of the Buddha, who discarded every question of cosmography as useless,[20] or even, for that matter, the Talmud, which, similarly, may have meant to sober up our curiosity when it disapproved of inquiry about what was before, what is underneath, and so on.[21]

As for the possibility of building a social order without referring to transcendence, I would like to qualify things. Not all religions want to foist on society a model of order. In particular, Christianity distinguishes itself from the former religions insofar as it doesn't impose on people rules of conduct other than the ones that natural, unaided reason either discovered or could have discovered. It leaves the content of the moral rules untouched and adds a further dimension only where morality can't save us.

This principle of subsidiarity of sorts explains at the same time why atheism has some trumps in its favor. For we have to account for the very possibility of atheism, and even for its plausibility. Now, it is the case that both subsidiarity and atheism can be deduced from the very character of the Christian God. To some extent, Christian theology can give an account of atheism. Islamic Kalām, on the other hand, is hard put to it when it endeavors to explain why some people don't believe, for the existence of a wise and all-powerful Creator is supposed to be self-evident. As a consequence, it can't be gainsaid if not by the willful obstinacy of "wicked" people, who refuse to yield to the witness of their intelligence. Atheism is not lack of insight, or any kind of tough luck; it is a lie, that is, a sin. For this reason, atheists lie outside the pale of mankind as "the worst of beasts" (Qur'an 8:22, my trans.), who can and must be done away with.

Saint Paul claims that God should be known by natural reason (Rom. 1:20), but the fact is that man doesn't always acknowledge him as Creator. Why is it that God is not evident? In order to answer, let me indulge in some anthropomorphism and ask what we can surmise of God's "intentions," what he is driving at. His aim is not making himself known. What he wants is not his own glory, for his glory would be his own good. And God doesn't look for his good. He *is* the Good. What he wants is to give himself to his creatures, thereby producing the good of his creatures. What we call God's "glory" is not his fame, but the very life of creation. Says the Greek church father Saint Irenaeus of Lyon (died ca. AD 202): "The glory of God is the living man" (*gloria Dei vivens homo*). God gives the creatures whatever is necessary for them to reach their own good by their own exertions. He reveals himself only when such a disclosure is necessary for a creature to do that. For this reason, Irenaeus's sentence goes on: "The life of man is the vision of God" (*vita hominis visio Dei*).[22]

We can illustrate this with a parable. When an unknown person asks us for directions, we give the right answer if we know, but we don't tell our name as long as we are simply asked about orientation. We give our name, or even our card, if, and only if, this can prove helpful. In the same way, God puts creation at the disposal of created beings themselves, and especially of man, who knows that there is such a thing as the world. But the created world doesn't clearly point toward the existence of a Creator. God reveals his name when this knowledge is instrumental to salvation: eternal life is such a "knowledge" (John 17:3).

When I had to choose a title for the present chapter, a phrase came to my mind: "the end of the tether." I would like to round it up by evoking two works whose titles include that image. The first is a thin pamphlet published in 1945, right after the end of the Second World War, by H. G. Wells under the title *Mind at the End of Its Tether*. The popular novelist and essay writer, who for a long time had written utopias on the future of an enlightened mankind freed from superstition by science and technology, bequeathed to us in his old age a gloomy view of the future. The only hope is that man should be replaced by an animal better fitted to the new conditions, unless a small minority of extremely pliable human beings survives.[23] The second one is the marvelous short novel, or long story, that Joseph Conrad published in 1902 under the plain title *The End of the Tether*. Captain Whalley, who is losing his eyesight, must go on sailing, for his daughter needs money. He keeps leading his ship till she finally suffers shipwreck. This might be read as a parable of the way in which atheism is steering Western culture.

CHAPTER THREE

The Necessity of Goodness

In a small book that I published some years ago, I observed that it might be apposite to have a closer look at the concept of the Good and to take it seriously. This would involve, as I said there, in a sense rehabilitating the Platonic conception of the Idea of the Good. We would thereby recant the way Aristotle put it aside.[1] All this remained a mere sketch and required some elaboration. Let me here take a further step in that direction.

We Are All Disciples of Aristotle

Let us spend some time with Aristotle, and we will be in pretty good company. For we will realize that, whenever the Good is at stake, we are still living on thoughts that are Aristotelian in origin. We share with Aristotle a basic assumption which is so deeply rooted in us that we don't identify it as such any longer.

It is well known that the disciple criticized his master Plato and observed that, for practical purposes, the Idea of the Good is useless for ethics. More useful is the *prakton agathon*, the Good that can be produced, that is, by us human beings.[2] That is, generally, Aristotle finds fault with Plato, who did not let the ideas work. The ideas are ideals, perhaps idols, but in any case idle.[3] Whereas concrete things act upon each other—whereas, for instance, to quote the ever-recurring example, "a human being begets a human being"[4]—the Platonic ideas stay in their heavens and twiddle their thumbs. Only the sun, in its most concrete sky, helps.[5] Says Kant somewhere: in contradistinction to Plato's flights of fancy, the philosophy of Aristotle is work.[6] The Stagirite was rather a manager, since he put the ideas in the things, expecting them to roll up their sleeves, spit in their hands, and produce something.

From this point of view, one could consider the Good as superfluous, as something merely decorative, as something that makes life more beautiful but that presupposes it. We would thereby remain in the wake of the Aristotelian distinction between living (*zēn*) and the living well (*eu zēn*). Aristotle says, for example: The political community comes into being for the sake of life, but it goes on existing for the sake of the good life.[7] To put it in Marxist parlance: Life *tout court*, as being alive (*zōē*) and as leading a life (*bios*), is the infrastructure; the Good is hardly more than a superstructure, something that sets a crown to life—in the same way as pleasure, according to another passage from Aristotle, is like the healthy glow that accompanies youth.[8] The Good is there as an adjective or an adverb rather than as a substantive.

In the same spirit, Aristotle distinguishes the use of the tongue for taste and for speaking, and in the same way the use of respiration for cooling the inner heat and for the voice. The former serve the Necessary; the latter exist for the Good.[9] Among perceptions, some cater to life, and some to the good life. This is the case of seeing and hearing, the higher senses that are capable of an aesthetic dimension.[10] Those that serve naked life are touch and the senses that depend on it, that is, taste and smelling. Touch alone is absolutely necessary for life, which depends on it.[11]

By this token, the Good is for sure a good thing—nobody gainsays that—but it is not necessary. Two cheers for the Good, but it is not the most urgent task.

The Good Can Wait

The secondary character of care for the Good comes from an old popular wisdom of the Greek people, which Aristotle and, before him, Plato tapped on. A saying was transmitted to us from the poet Phokylides, a Milesian of the early sixth century before Christ: "We should look for a living, then for virtue, but only after one has got a living" (dizēsthai biotēn, aretēn d', hotan ēi bios ēdē), to which Plato explicitly alludes.[12] The same view is expressed in many proverbs, for example *primum vivere, deinde . . . philosophari* (first, you have to live; philosophy comes afterward) or anything else.[13] Nowadays, we take for granted that "it's the economy, stupid!," and virtue is optional. But the most outspoken statement may be the one that Machiavelli puts into the mouth of a leader of the Ciompi, who revolted in Florence in 1378: "We have no business thinking about conscience; for when people such as we have to fear hunger, and imprisonment, or death, the fear of hell neither can nor ought to have any influence upon them."[14] One can find everywhere stronger and more cynical versions of the same—for instance in Bertolt Brecht, whose "first comes the grub, then morals"[15] is in all mouths.

Behind all this, the basic assumption which I earlier alluded to is that the good is something that we *do*. As a consequence, we can do the good or fail to do it. From time to time, we have to let it go provisionally, by postponing it to the future. As the object of *praxis*, it belongs to the realm of practical philosophy, especially to the branch that deals with the actions of people, to wit, morals. Since the Good is an ethical concept, little wonder that we took our bearings from Aristotle's *Ethics*.

The Good as Something Necessary

Now, let me ask a question: What if the Good is a condition of life, and an absolutely necessary one into the bargain? Such a thesis is not brand new. On the contrary, it retrieves in a new way a hoary assumption that ancient and medieval metaphysics borrowed from Plato. Let me first rapidly sketch it before I attempt the revamping that it so badly needs.

There is a most classic way to ground the necessity of the Good. It consists in extolling it and, conversely, in lowering its contrary, that is, the Bad, on the scale of being. What is worse occupies on this ladder a lower rung than what is better and possesses, so to speak, a weaker intensity of being. This is a solution that is to be found, for example, in Boethius, who bequeathed it to the whole Latin Middle Ages.[16] This presupposes that the

Good and Being wax and wane together, that they sort of run parallel to each other. We easily recognize here the scholastic doctrine of the convertibility of the transcendental properties, especially of Being (*Ens*) and the Good (*Bonum*): *ens et bonum convertuntur* (Being and Good stand for each other).[17] If every being, as such, is good, then the presence of the Good is necessary wherever there is something, that is, everywhere. The Good may even stretch further than Being, as in Dionysius the Areopagite.[18] But this would lead us too far.

I agree to the doctrine of the convertibility of the Good with Being up to a point, but it is so recondite and far from our present day that I should like to make it more plausible by proceeding indirectly. A simple way opens itself, if we follow the ethical enterprise to its end, in thought as well as in action. Human freedom is something that ethics presupposes and fosters in its turn. The foundation of morals by Kant shows this situation with great clarity. Ethical life is free if and only if it holds in check the influence of external agents—that is, of all that Kant calls "pathological"—for the benefit of an action that obeys its own laws, and hence deserves to be called "autonomous." Yet one presupposes that action comes from a subject that is already there.

The Subject

Now this subject is a rational being in general. It must be rational for it to be able to act. Not any motion is an action. A stone that rolls down a steep slope doesn't act. Neither does the plant that grows, pushes its roots deep in the earth, and unfolds its boughs. Whether an animal "acts," properly speaking, is not clear. "Acting" means rather implementing a course of action that one has planned and wanted (*prohairesis*), both with freedom. By this token, Aristotle could contend that animals that are driven by their instinct don't act.[19] Even human beings can hardly be said to act when their gestures are triggered by reflexes, for instance when we withdraw our hand from a burning stove.

Kant underlines explicitly, and even with insistence, that the subjects that abide by the moral law are not necessarily human beings, but rational beings in general. In the second *Critique*, Kant harps upon the theme. The clearest passage may be the second note to the "Fundamental Law of the Pure Practical Reason": "This principle of morality . . . is declared by the reason to be a law for all rational beings, insofar as they have a will, that is, a power to determine their causality by the conception of rules. . . . It is, therefore, not limited to men only, but applies to all finite beings that possess reason and will; it even includes the Infinite Being as the supreme intelligence."[20] There is an interesting parallel in Kant's theoretical philosophy, for, in the same way, the first *Critique* refused to "limit the mode of intuition in space and time to the sensuous faculty of man. It may well be that all finite thinking beings must necessarily in this respect agree with man (though as to this we cannot decide)."[21] Despite his admiration and respect for Kant, Schopenhauer poked fun at the idea and wrote with a sneer that Kant probably thought of the nice little angels.[22] He was driving the nail home, perhaps even more than he thought. This is what is shown elsewhere by Kant.

Angels

In this passage, the Prussian philosopher writes that the problem of building a political constitution is in principle soluble, even if the citizens are devils, provided those devils are rational.[23] If only they listen to the reckonings of their calculating reason, those utterly wicked creatures can understand that it is in their interest to live in peace with each other. Kant exaggerates thereby the paradox that David Hume expressed one generation earlier, namely that politicians should take their bearings from the assumption that "every man must be supposed a knave," which is, says the Scottish philosopher, a wise and politically most effective maxim.[24] Much earlier, Augustine had alluded to the fact: gangsters, too, abide by some laws, if they want to build a lasting gang, in order correctly to ply their criminal trade.[25] Modern thinkers generalized: every human society is a pack of wolves or a gang of criminals.

Now, one may ask whether Kant did not make his task too light, whether he in fact chose a simpler case while giving the impression of choosing to scrutinize a more difficult one. To be sure, the case of the devils is actually trickier, because they are so utterly bad: you can't expect the ghost of a good intention when they proceed to set up their pandemonium and to write a constitution for it. But this is only one side of the coin. The flip side is that, by choosing devilish beings as an example, one shirks the question of the temporal existence of human beings and of its consequences. As fallen angels, but angels all the same, devils float in what Greeks called *aiōn*, and the Romans *aevum*, that is, indefinitely long duration; as such they outsoar physical and biological existence. Among other things, they shirk the necessity to reproduce in order to go on existing as a species. Each devil, the same as every good angel, is his own species.

These considerations on pure spirits may sound arbitrary, and even otiose. Yet it might be the case that pondering them awhile, as a thought experiment, might shed some light on our present predicament. In his book on the leading minds of modern times, Jacques Maritain observed that Descartes lifted the human intellect up to a place that classical metaphysics saved for the angelic intellect.[26] Whether this holds true in the case of Descartes, I doubt. Nevertheless, the hint is valuable for every student of modern thought. It looks as if its categories were tailored for angels rather than for human beings.

Freedom as a Principle

The proud self-image of modern thought puts freedom in the center of the human. For Hegel, "the history of the world is none other than the progress of the consciousness of freedom."[27] In the overall framework of history, modern times, which begin according to Hegelian parlance immediately after the fall of the Roman Empire, occupy a particularly important place as the epoch in which freedom was discovered as a principle that holds true for all human beings. This took place with the rise of Christianity and the entry of Germanic people onto the stage. Again Hegel: "The right of the subject's particularity, his right to be satisfied, or in other words the right of subjective freedom, is the hub and center of the difference between antiquity and modern times. This right in its infinity is given expression in Christianity, and it has become the universal working principle of a new form of civilization."[28] We only have to follow till the end the consequences of this principle which lies at the very basis of action, hence of morality. This is actually what the movement of modern times wanted to do. If one prolongs its direction, one reaches the point where totally free beings call themselves into existence. Radical autonomy then is some sort of self-creation.

And here, we meet again our friends the angelic beings. According to the most classical theory of orthodox theology, devils are fallen angels.[29] As pure, bodiless spirits, the angelic hosts were set into being by God, but they had to decide, right after their creation, whether they would understand themselves as thankfully turned toward God or dream of an independence vis-à-vis their Creator. A devil becomes what he is—that is, a bad and fallen angel—through an act of freedom, in the same way as good angels distinguish themselves from the apostates only through the fact that they freely accept God's creative love. This happened in a decision of freedom that took place in an instant[30] but made them forever what they are. The devil is not self-begotten, contrary to Satan's boast in Milton.[31] Like every angel, it is God's creature, but it makes itself to what it is—that is, a devil—through an act of free will, exactly as the good angels freely choose to obey God.

We human beings can, as a matter of course only up to a point, choose the properties that we want to give to ourselves, for instance our walk of life, our job, our partner in marriage, and so on. Says Kierkegaard: We don't create ourselves, we only choose ourselves.[32] Analogically to the angel, man has to acknowledge in himself an element of passivity, since he can't possibly deny his biological basis, let alone cast it away. Nevertheless, in modern times, man toys with the idea of weighing the anchors and of reaching a total self-determination that would make him some sort of quasi-angel.

Birth

Let us now come down from the angels to the lower level that we, human beings, occupy. For the question is still there, how action takes place in the concrete case that interests us, because it concerns us directly, that is, in the case where the acting subjects are human beings of flesh and blood.

The concrete subjects with whom we interact, and even the subjects who we are, were born in some place and at some time. Now, birth is an event which is not determined by its subject, since he/she is not yet extant. It represents an extreme case of heteronomy, since it doesn't affect only *what* a being is, but the very fact *that* it is. Whether I exist, that is what other people decided for me. Being born is not an action that could arise from a subject, but that which furnishes any action with its subject.

Furthermore, our birth as individuals of the species *Homo sapiens* is hardly more than the last event in a series that harks back to the very beginning of life in the "warm little pond" which Darwin talked about.[33] It even reaches as far as the so-called Big Bang, since physicists tell us that the atoms out of which our body consists were made only some moments after the beginning.

One thinks of Hannah Arendt's concept of "natality," which she very consciously puts forward as a counterpart to the grim obsession of the philosophers with mortality.[34] Now, this concept views the phenomenon in a somewhat unilateral way. Whereas it underscores the possibility of making a new beginning, it obfuscates the aspect of pure passivity that being born unmistakably possesses, and this aspect is precisely that which natality has in common with mortality. One is familiar with the hackneyed lines of Rilke:

> O Lord, give each of us our own death.
> A dying that is born to each life,
> our own desire, our purpose, love, dearth.[35]

Now, we are allowed to ask: Whose death should we die, if not our own? Furthermore, we should ask whether we could speak, in a way symmetrical to Rilke's lines on death, of "being born into one's own birth." Looking for an "authentic" way of being born hardly makes sense. My birth is necessarily my own, not the birth of another person—say, my brother. But my "Mine-ness" (*Jemeinigkeit*)—to use Heidegger's parlance in the very apt translation by Bettina Bergo—shows paradoxical features, insofar as the "I" to whom this event happens can't claim any preexistence, but is made real or possible by this very event.

Shame

This intertwining of autonomy and radical heteronomy, this clash of two irreconcilable contraries, produces a feeling of unpleasantness. According to a rather cryptic sentence of Emmanuel Levinas, "Birth, which we don't choose and can't possibly choose, is the great drama of contemporary thought."[36]

One already has observed to what extent modern man is, in a sense, ashamed of being merely human, so that he dreams of becoming more than simply human. On the shame, Dostoyevsky wrote as early as 1864 at the end of his enigmatic *Notes from the Underground*: "We are oppressed at being men—men with a real individual body and blood, we are ashamed of it, we think it a disgrace and try to contrive to be some sort of impossible generalized man [общечеловек, obšetšelovek]."[37] Dostoyevsky was certainly not a philosopher, but his last utterance can be transposed in a philosophical key, as follows: the shocking thing is individuation, the fact that we received our own particular body—the matter of which individualizes us—and not another one. We would be glad to possess the same universality as the angels, since each and every one of them is his own species. We could as well think of the concept, introduced by Günter Anders, of a "Promethean shame," through which man is ashamed not to be a match against the perfection of his own products.[38] The artifacts are perfect because they were designed and made according to a preexisting blueprint, not begotten and born.

On the dream of becoming something more, Nietzsche turns king's evidence, with the wish he expresses in his Zarathustra to overcome man and to sail in the direction of the Overman.[39] Today, the dreams or nightmares of a posthuman coming to a head of human history are deeply rooted in the nostalgia of modern man. Hence the fascination exerted upon our contemporaries by the so-called transhumanist project of a metamorphosis of human beings into beings that would be more than human.

Our Access to the Good

What can we do with this radical impossibility of doing anything that our being born brings with it? What kind of ethics could obtain in a domain in which any action is simply impossible? In so thin an air, the name of ethics, as care for what is good, wouldn't be apposite any longer. Yet, on the other hand, there exists the possibility of an "extramoral" access to the Good.

This access appears as the necessary ground or infrastructure of life as soon as we realize that there is a point on which freedom as the condition of action and the radical nonfreedom of birth meet, and even clash against each other. This point is generation. The existence of humankind depends on the free decision of its members, and it does that all the more as technology progresses. Instinct may vouch for the survival of animal species. In the case of man, it is more and more pushed back and relayed by freedom. This submission of natural impulses is a fact that we must wholeheartedly condone but, mind you, only if it brings the subject of freedom to self-*assertion*, not to self-*destruction*. Now, for this we need an external fulcrum.

Plato conceived of the Good not so much as a norm which active subjects have to abide by, but rather as a creative principle. He compares the Idea of the Good with the sun. Now Plato insists that the sun doesn't only pour its light on what already is (for example, to show human beings the right path), but gives being and life to what doesn't exist yet. It furnishes coming-to-be (*genesis*), growing (*auxē*), and food (*trophē*).[40] This corresponds to our everyday experience: the sun makes plants grow, brings again the spring and love-season of animals, and so on. Aristotle concurred with the utterance which I alluded to at the beginning of this chapter, that is, "a human being begets a human being—with the help of the sun."[41] What he unmistakably understood in a literal—that is, material—sense can be interpreted as a metaphor for the necessity of the Good for the survival of man.

The biblical idea of creation takes its bearings from the same assumption about goodness as a principle of whatever exists. The first narrative of creation in Genesis even culminates in the assertion of the goodness of being (1:31). This link between creation and goodness is important because the idea of creation doesn't involve goodness as such. Some extrabiblical accounts of the way in which a powerful being brings about the world simply ignore the axiological ranking of what is created, or even give it a negative value. According to the authors whom we put under the heading of "Gnostics," the world is the work either of an incompetent bungler or of a cruel craftsman who wanted to build a jail for the souls fallen from some superior realm of pure spirits.[42] For modern deists, the world can be said in a certain rather loose sense to be created, but the idea that the creative principle cares for what it creates is absent.

David Hume toyed with the idea of an imperfect world bearing witness to the only relative perfection of its creator.[43] By this token, goodness and creation don't necessarily belong together. Their connection is the good news implied by both Plato and the Bible.

How can I tolerate not having created myself? My answer is, if and only if I come from some utterly good principle. Suppose that I owe my being to chance, that is, to the concourse of blind forces. If a "blind watchmaker" (R. Dawkins)[44] threw me into life without asking me for advice, why should I play the same dirty trick on other people, by inoculating them with life? If, on the contrary, I feel myself and my fellow beings as the creatures of a good and generous God who calls us to partake of his own loving life, then I have excellent reasons to ensure the continuance of life.

Nature

What we inhabit—individually as well as insofar as we are part of a living species and of a social construct—what we draw upon in order to go on living, the total show that we contemplate, all this we have been for a long time calling by the name of "Nature." With the modern era, Nature has become less and less our house and more and more a field that we till, a tank of energy which we tap, or at best a landscape in which we have our Sunday strolls when we don't exploit the same as a quarry or a mine during the week. The meaning of our presence inside of nature, and even of our being to some extent a part of it, disappears behind our activity of exploiting it or our leisure in it. Retrieving it might be the task of a philosophy of nature, a discipline that we badly need.

An Urgent Need

Now, this notion has a long and winding story behind it, and it would be apposite first to sketch it, in order to distinguish its former concrete realizations from the kind of philosophy of nature whose existence I am wishing for. Let me here sum up this story under three headings, three possible meanings of the phrase.

(1) *First, there is "natural philosophy"* (philosophia naturalis), such as is still taught in Cambridge, from the chair once occupied by Isaac New-

ton, a chair that has kept its original name. We mean thereby physics as a description of natural things, together with the writing of their laws in rigorous mathematical language.

(2) *Second, there is the inquiry concerning the basic concepts of natural science*: to begin with, nature, motion, time, space, matter, or whatnot. This was the main subject matter of Aristotle's *Physics*. I wholeheartedly condone such an enterprise.

Yet both endeavors are tasks which science either doesn't need or can't cope with very successfully on its own. Science very well can shift for itself without the aid of philosophy. It has been doing that for centuries, roughly speaking since Galileo, and it keeps developing exponentially. Philosophy could only encumber science with its help or plume itself with results which it has not toiled to get.

(3) *A third meaning is the* Naturphilosophie *that was a catchword and a program for German idealism.* Its concrete results in Schelling and Hegel were, to say the least, hardly convincing. Yet this brings us nearer to what I dream of. For such an endeavor arose from the consciousness of a problem: How can we articulate to each other the physical world and what singles out man, that is, the moral dimension and the sensitivity to values? Kant pointed toward this problem with his idea of beauty as a symbol of morality.[1] Fichte, in the wake of Kant's primacy of practical reason, endeavored to deduce the very existence of the physical world from the requirements of moral action.[2]

The underlying enigma is the possibility of those weird beings, known as "human beings," who, alone among animals, possess a feeling for the Good and for the Beautiful.

The leading question of a philosophy of nature such as I wish to have and, to repeat, that I could not possibly produce, would deal with our own presence in nature as human beings. It would involve not an anthropology that would be one among other descriptions of natural things, the thing at stake being man, but a reflexive understanding of the part we play in the whole show.

Wanted: Cosmology

In a former book that hails back from more than fifteen years already, I put forward the thesis that we don't possess a cosmology any longer.[3]

I meant thereby an intellectual pursuit different from two other ones, both belonging to science, that is, cosmography and cosmogony. Cosmography, as the name suggests, describes (*graphein*) the present state of affairs in the physical universe. Cosmogony endeavors to reconstruct the way in which this state of affairs became (*gignesthai*) what it is now.

In the classical, late antique, and medieval model, which had superseded the emergence myths, there was little room for a cosmogony. Plato's *Timaeus*, which describes how a powerful Craftsman designed and produced the world, was quickly interpreted as a pedagogical device meant to make the structure of an eternal state of affairs more easily understandable. The Aristotelian model of an eternal and unchanging world dominated late antique and Arabic philosophy in the wake of Proclus. In Latin Europe, the comeback of Aristotle's physics and astronomy in the late twelfth century and its reception by Scholastic thinkers relegated to the realm of literature the attempts of the Chartres School at harmonizing Plato and Genesis.

After the astronomic revolution of the sixteenth and seventeenth centuries, a new cosmography arose, which gave a satisfactory description of the present structure of the world. But its genesis was shrouded in mystery and remained so in spite of various hypotheses, for instance the one of Kant, later taken up by Laplace. Early modern times had a cosmography, but no cosmogony. Those two realms, which remained separated for more than three centuries, were brought together by people like Arthur Eddington, Edwin Hubble, Fr. Georges Lemaître, and others. We are at present in possession of a powerful model, known by the moniker of the Big Bang theory. This model becomes more and more plausible as the amount of our knowledge increases. To be sure, since scientific knowledge is essentially provisional, nobody knows how long it will last.

In contradistinction to both endeavors, I take here the word "cosmology" in the meaning that is suggested by its etymology: a *logos* about the *kosmos*. Not a mere description, but some sort of account, an attempt at making sense of it, at deciphering its meaning.

Here one may ask whether such an enterprise is really useful. It would not add a whit to our scientific knowledge of nature if by "cosmology" we mean nothing more than our ability to discover nature's laws, let alone if we mean merely our technical grip on nature. But the question remains whether what we have to do with nature can boil down to knowing it and taking advantage of it for our own purposes—in other words, the question to what extent nature is *interesting* for us.[4]

No Logos of Nature

We can write the laws of the physical universe in the precise and rigorous language of mathematics, but we don't *understand* this universe in the strict meaning of "understanding." Nature can be described very accurately, and we can on the basis of this description perform many technical wonders. But nature can't be understood any longer. Understanding supposes that we introduce final causes. I understand what a person is doing when she throws a letter into a mailbox because I know that her intention is that her message be carried to her friend. Now, final causes have no place in the study of the physical world. They have been expelled since Francis Bacon's quip comparing them to consecrated virgins who remain barren.[5] Scientists are perfectly right to do without them, and even to do away with them, since their admission would let in an illegitimate kind of anthropomorphism.

Attempts at reintroducing final causes are commonly frowned upon by scientists, and short lived. Final causes can be tolerated in the study of living organisms, for want of anything better, as long as we haven't yet found the mechanism that accounts for what we want to explain. This is the careful stand taken by Kant in his third *Critique*.[6] The lack of final causes and, as its consequence, the impossibility of really understanding the world are not a problem for science. But they are one for us as human beings, since, as such, we experience the world through human minds, and hence can't do without some sort of anthropomorphism.

Ancient philosophy, which comprised a rudimentary description of physical phenomena, furnished us with an understanding of nature. Heavy bodies fall and light bodies go upward because they strive to reach their natural abodes, where they find their specific fulfillment, that is, their good.[7] Modern physics has gotten rid of this explanation. We are caught between an explanation that we can't accept any longer and a description that doesn't allow us to understand anything. To be sure, schizophrenia is a mental state that mankind can live with for a long time without pangs of conscience. It did that for centuries, for instance when the mathematical hypotheses of Ptolemaic astronomy on the one hand and on the other hand Aristotelian physics, which refute each other, coexisted.

By this token, the trouble is that the scientific worldview makes of us *strangers* in the cosmos. It expels man from the world[8] and thereby fosters the danger of a revival of the Gnostic attitude. The presence of Gnosticism in modern thought has been diagnosed by several thinkers already, for instance Eric Voegelin in his famous Walgren Lectures of 1953, later published under the title *The New Science of Politics.*[9] Gnostic "science" was bogus. Augustine, for instance, was deeply disappointed by the Manichaean account of the structure of the physical universe and left the Manichaean church for this reason. But real science has Gnostic consequences.

Modern man is at the same time a castaway and an upstart. Since he is the former, he has to become the latter. As a castaway, he uses makeshift implements to build a raft of sorts, floating on an ocean of chaos. As for the upstart, let us here indulge in some cheap psychology. A true-blue gentleman, intimately convinced of his innate superiority over the ragtag and bobtail, can be exquisitely polite and modest toward other people. On the other hand, a person without nobility, in Latin *sine nobilitate—snob.*, for short—has to be a snob. Precisely because he doubts his own legitimacy, he will have to make others feel his alleged superiority; he will despise them, and even lord it over them. To the best of my knowledge, the most illuminating study on the dialectics of snobbishness was provided by René Girard in his very first book. He explains how modern, democratic societies are in a way compelled to reintroduce hierarchies by artificial ways once hierarchies that were allegedly "natural" were demoted. Hence the clubs, the practice of blackballing candidates whom the older members wish to avoid rubbing shoulders with, and so on.[10]

Modern man is such a snob. He is that way not only in his social life among his fellow human beings but in his relationship to being at large as well. He is unsure of his legitimacy and working hard in order to be admitted into the club to which he belongs as its only member, looking down at the other natural beings and trying to subdue them. This is what we have been doing for four centuries, as a program, since Bacon's clarion call and, through technology, since the industrial revolution.

There is another aspect to that, quite practical. We are in a double double bind, a Catch-22 (or -44?) of sorts as for the way in which we understand ourselves and the way we understand nature. As for ourselves, on the one hand, contemporary science, or rather the ideological use made of it by the mainstream media, leads us to believe that we are hardly more than lucky monkeys, produced by the chance encounter of irrational forces. On the other hand, we harp upon the "dignity" of man, endowed with "human rights" that are supposed to provide us with the unshakable ground for our moral choices and legal rulings. Little wonder that some people propose to enlarge the notion of rights to animals, since human beings themselves are conceived of as animals that happen to be endowed, nobody knows why, with sacred and unalienable rights. As for nature, on the one hand, we can see nature (lowercase "n") as a mere fuel tank, a quarry of useful materials, at our beck and call, and even as materials that we can reshape as we wish. On the other hand, we can worship Nature (capital "N") as a goddess. This was the case for the eighteenth-century *Philosophes*, or again for some deep ecologists, who even recycled for the earth the Greek name Gaia. The part played by the earth in this worldview gives us an inkling of what such worship could produce. All idols require human sacrifices. To Gaia's welfare, mankind, the troublemaker, should be sacrificed

Hence, we need a balanced view of nature that would steer a middle course between those two pairs of extremes.

Nature in the Bible

Leo Strauss was perfectly right to point out that the basic concept of the philosophical enterprise in its whole, the concept by which it stands and without which it falls, is the concept of nature. It arose first in Greek philosophical thought, when it disentangled itself from earlier forms of thought, like myth. He was right, too, to observe that the concept is nowhere to be met with in the text of the other pillar of Western culture, the Hebrew Bible.[11] The word for "nature," *teva'*, does occur in both Talmuds, under the pen of medieval thinkers,[12] and is common in present-day Israeli Ivrit. But it is not to be found earlier than the Mishnah, in the second century of the Christian era. Furthermore, it has lost its connection with the representation of a spontaneous growth that the Greek expressed by means of the dubious popular etymology of *physis* (φύσις)—already present in Aristotle—according to which it derived from *phyein* (φύειν), "to grow."[13] Instead of that, *teva'* refers rather to the trace left on wax by a seal ring.[14]

There is no concept of nature in the Bible because there is in it no concept whatsoever. "Nature" is no exception. Yet a concept may be present in a narrative form. By this token, the concept of nature is present in an implicit way in the first account of creation:

> The earth brought forth vegetation, plants yielding seed according to their own kinds, and trees bearing fruit in which is their seed, each according to its kind. . . . God created the great sea creatures and every living creature that moves, with which the waters swarm, according to their kinds, and every winged bird according to its kind. . . . And God said, "Let the earth bring forth living creatures according to their kinds—livestock and creeping things and beasts of the earth according to their kinds." And it was so. And God made the beasts of the earth according to their kinds and the livestock according to their kinds, and everything that creeps on the ground according to its kind. (Gen. 1:12, 21, 24–25 ESV)

Whatever is is created after its kind (*le-mīn* + possessive pronoun), not as a loose bundle of species, things, or properties. Each creature possesses its own inner structure and stays in being in the limits of this species. Reproduction takes place according to the species of the individual that reproduces itself by begetting its match. Aristotle would have seen in this expression a poetical formulation of the principle of what is natural, a rule that he sets forth many times in the formula "man begets man."[15]

Two features catch the eye in this first account of creation: on the one hand, the fact that creation depends on a speech act, a *davar* that will become a *logos* in the Greek version, and on the other hand that the act of creating sets into being a system of natures that are neatly distinguished from, as well as articulated on, one another. Those two striking features most probably are two sides of the same coin. I can't expatiate on this here, but let me remind you of the recurrent images that we see in the creation narrative with its carefully crafted structure, the analogue of a poem.[16] This view of creation lies at the ground of the medieval worldview.

The Medieval Outlook Helpful

Now, my claim is that what we need in order to meet the challenges of our time is something like the medieval outlook.[17] The core fact is, in my view, that medieval thinkers did not experience the world as nature (*physis*) any longer, but as creation. This feeling was so spontaneous that, most interestingly, Saint Bernard distinguished somewhere between creature in general (*creatura aliqua*) and creature of God (*creatura Dei*), parallel to the distinction between nature (*natura*) and grace (*gratia*).[18] This distinction, which at first blush sounds preposterous (for whose creation could there be, if not God's?), might have been hardly more than a rhetorical ploy, but it shows how deeply rooted the vision of being as created was ingrained in medieval minds.

We need the idea of creation. The trouble is that this word has been polluted by the use made of it by the so-called creationism that relies on a naively literal reading of the first account of creation in Genesis, a reading that was scarcely to be found among the church fathers. Augustine's literal commentary on Genesis, for instance, doesn't object to the idea of a progressive development in the course of time of abilities sown by God on the first day.[19] By the way, Darwin toyed with this idea in the last sentence of his first masterpiece.[20] Whether he sincerely admitted the idea or only wanted to blunt the edges of his theory in order to make it more palatable for Victorian religious sensitivity is another story.

The idea of creation doesn't tell us anything about the synchronic structure of beings, that is, cosmography, or about the diachronic process of their unfolding, that is, cosmogony. God has endowed us with the intellectual tools we'll need by and by to acquire an adequate knowledge of those beings. But the idea of creation teaches us a basic truth about the existence of what is, to wit, that it is not out of itself (*a se*).

In order for us better to learn this truth and to draw its consequences, the work of Aquinas could be a great help, for several reasons. Let us group them under two headings, one general, the other peculiar to him.

In other words, he could help us first because he is medieval, and second because he is himself. Being a man of the Middle Ages, Aquinas shares the basic assumptions of the medieval worldview. Being the theological and philosophical genius that he was, he sifted this worldview and recast it in conceptual terms.

One advantage of the medieval worldview and in particular of Aquinas's outlook is paradoxical in nature. I mean that his cosmography is desperately outdated and could not possibly be made up-to-date. It is basically Aristotle's worldview, or the framework which Ptolemy in his astronomy, Galen in his psychology, and other scientists filled with a more elaborate content. Hence, the temptation of trying to rejuvenate his cosmography on the scientific level can easily be staved off and, together with it, any attempt at so-called concordism, a naive effort at finding scientific data of astronomy, physics, or biology hidden in the sacred books.

Let me give just one example of the medieval view of nature. I will borrow it from the poets, who as a rule are more adept at expressing the basic assumptions of a culture than philosophers or scientists. According to the poets, the birds have a language of their own. The idea is a relatively common one, in Europe as well as in the Persian world and probably elsewhere. But it is interesting to point out that the language of the birds' chirruping is not just any language. It has a name. It is Latin. For the first time, perhaps, the Provençal poet William IX of Aquitaine, in the second half of the twelfth century, wrote that the morning birds sing "each one in its Latin" (*chascus en lor lati*). The phrase became trite in French, Italian, and English; it is to be found as late as in the Russian poet Ossip Mandelstam (d. 1938), who probably borrowed it from one of the medieval poets whom he was so fond of.[21] For the poets, this probably meant that we can't understand the birds, and "Latin" can mean, in other contexts, language in general. But we are allowed to take this literally. The birds don't speak just any vernacular, but the dignified language of higher administration and culture, the language of the Roman Empire and of its classical writers. The troubadour Arnaut Daniel adds a detail: in their Latin, the birds say their prayers.[22] Although, for the poet, this prayer is directed to their mates, this is very much in keeping with the old idea of the Neoplatonist philosophers: "Whatever exists prays, with the exception of the First."[23] Church fathers concurred, and even, in the case of Gregory of Nazianzus, took up the same wording: "All things pray to You."[24]

We can take the birds as a metonymy for Nature at large. Natural things have a meaning. They are not only just there, at our disposal, but can convey a message and become our teachers. There is more to this idea than a naive theory of allegory in the bestiaries: the ant as a model of assiduity at work, the pelican as a figure of Christ's sacrifice, and so on. What this "more" means, Aquinas will help us understand.

Aquinas's View of Created Nature

Aquinas as such, I contend, can help us in the formidable task of reconstructing a philosophy of nature. Let me choose two points only, one dealing with nature herself, one with our studying her.

As for the first one, Aquinas looks at creation as having as its object not bundles of properties floating somewhere but things that have a stable nature of their own. God is the creator of natures, an idea that is already to be found in Augustine and earlier.[25] Now, this is far from being self-evident. Whoever supports the idea of creation is not committed to conceive of the objects which are created as being full-fledged *things*. Islam powerfully upholds the idea of creation, but Islamic thinkers of the so-called *Kalām* (*Mutakallimūn*) don't view it as dealing with things. This holds good especially for the school of al-Ašʿarī, which carried the day and kept a dominant position almost to the present day, whereas some other authors, like Ibn Hazm, went near to the idea of a God who created natures.[26] This school stood for a radical atomistic worldview, not only as for the structure of matter but as for time, supposed to consist of instants, and, more important still, as for the very structure of being. Beings consist of bundles of properties. By developing such a view, the followers of al-Ašʿarī did away with the idea of nature. They replaced it with the idea of God's "habit" (*ʿāda*) of creating some properties together.

The Jewish philosopher Moses Maimonides dealt this view a mortal blow in his community.[27] This did not prevent later Christian authors like Malebranche—who by the way were indirectly influenced by the Islamic Kalām—from seeing in Nature a pagan idea.[28] As for Aquinas, he took over Rabbi Moses's critique and summed up his own view in magnificent and famous formulas, such as the following: "Demeaning the perfection of creatures amounts to demeaning the perfection of God's power" (Detrahere . . . perfectioni creaturarum est detrahere perfectioni divinae virtutis).[29]

Created things have stable properties, and they have their own laws, which enable us to get a scientific knowledge of their functioning. Modern science might have been made possible by the intellectual breakthroughs of late "nominalist" thinkers like Nicole Oresme or Jean Buridan, not to mention the earlier John Philoponus (sixth century). This is the well-known thesis of the French physicist and historian Pierre Duhem.[30] But, earlier than that, the idea of stable natures set into being by the creative act was at least a necessary, if not a sufficient, condition of natural science.

What the philosophically trained Scholastic authors expressed in conceptual terms came to the fore as well, and even earlier, in the image of Nature as God's viceroy, his vicarious helper in shaping the variety of living beings. The authors of the so-called School of Chartres, in the twelfth century, most probably, coined this image for the first time, perhaps on the basis of their reading of Boethius and of what was available to them of Plato's *Timaeus*. In any case, the earliest occurrence that I could spot is to be found in a prose part of a didactic prosimetron by Alain of Lille (Alanus ab Insulis) around 1160. He does not hesitate to call Nature "vice-God" (*prodea*). In the thirteenth century, the image was taken up by Jean de Meung, the second author of the *Roman de la rose*. Finally, at the very end of the fourteenth century, it was quoted almost literally by Chaucer in his *Canterbury Tales*.[31]

So much for the first point, that is, the ontological status of created things.

Why Study Nature?[32]

As for our study of nature, mankind has been plying it eagerly for centuries, but the question why we do that was seldom asked. When asked, Westerners would off the cuff answer by pointing to the benefits of a technical control over natural phenomena, made possible by the knowledge of their mechanism.

Now, Aquinas explains why we should study nature—he says *consideratio*, to consider nature—why it is useful for the instruction of the faith.[33] He adduces several reasons and even includes with a poker face a quotation by Augustine, whose nose of wax he turns in his own direction, back to front. As for positive reasons, studying nature gives us an inkling of God's attributes, his wisdom and power. It even makes us somehow similar to him. Thomas adds four negative reasons, three of them ways that the study of nature helps us avoid errors about God: it helps us avoid mistaking him for a body, ascribing to the influence of creatures what God alone can do, and conversely subtracting from God's action what is his own. A fourth reason is especially interesting for us: Aquinas insists that a sober view of nature prevents us from yielding to the temptation to lower the level of our own being. In his time and age, this meant in particular lowering ourselves by submitting our freedom to astrological determinism. What is avoided by the study of nature is whatever detracts from human dignity (*hominum derogant dignitati*).[34] Thomas is—strange bedfellows—near to Epicurus, who explained that studying nature, ultimately, has no other relevance than doing away with every possible source of unease of the mind. Tranquility as absence of trouble (*ataraxia*), as the state of the mind which no wind ruffles (*galēnē*), is something that Greek wisdom strove after.

But dignity is more than peace of mind. We could even say that the consciousness of one's dignity might be the best warrant for real tranquility. And here, we are better equipped to meet the requirements of the modern attitude toward life and nature. I mentioned above the way in which the upstart must become a busybody, eager to compensate for his innate inferiority by working like a beaver, in contradistinction to the peaceful, somehow lackadaisical nonchalance of the authentic nobleman. If human beings were convinced of their own dignity, they would feel less of a need to compensate by muscling into nature's larder and pillaging it.

CHAPTER FIVE

Freedom and Creation

We are present among natural beings as some sort of aliens, endowed with a property which we share with no other earthly being, that is, freedom. Freedom is what singles out man as a rational living being. Hence the importance of our getting clearer ideas of its origin and meaning. In a former paper, I tried to dig out the roots of our Western idea of freedom which lie buried in the Bible.[1] Let me now look at it from a more philosophical point of view, thereby in a way complementing "Jerusalem" with "Athens," but not leaving the first city totally. I will first sketch our present confusion about freedom, then collect several uses of the adjective "free." Finally, I will consider the way in which a full-fledged view of freedom should recapitulate a great many of those uses.

Our Present-Day Confusion about Freedom

It is apposite that we should endeavor to shed light on the idea of freedom, because we witness a great deal of confusion on this topic in the present day.

When we were young lads, we would hurl to the face of our parents or teachers: "I will do what I want!" Now, sobering up, we realize that this was quite a tall order. . . . For, more often than not, rather than do, we *are done to* and do what another party wants us to do. Who or what exactly wants us to do things may vary: tradition, habit, advertisement, social pressure, the media, and so on. We realize that our parents and teachers and all kinds of visible authorities played a far smaller part in shaping our opinions than all those less visible and more insidious agents. The most efficient pressure is not external tyranny, which can only win external following and be paid lip service to. It is a "soft power" that sort of buys our willingness to comply.

In my country, and in other ones, too, like Spain, when a cab is for hire and looking for a customer, it has a flag of sorts on which is written "free." For many of our contemporaries, the model of what "being free" means is the way in which this cab is "free." This means that it is empty, that it doesn't go to any particular place, and can be taken over and hired by anybody who can pay. The same ambiguity can be observed not only in the case of the static concept of freedom but in the case of the dynamic notion of "liberation." Let us take "liberation of sexuality," a phrase supposed to summarize the evolution of Western mores, especially in the sixties. When I hear it, I can't help immediately thinking of the "liberation" of nuclear energy, together with its consequences, be they positive or negative. When I hear the title of the TV series *Sex and the City*, to my ears it sounds like the "Manhattan Project."

In the political realm, we are proud of our free institutions, and have a right to be. They warrant the social and political implementation of freedom as liberty. But they are more often than not—and, I feel this in my bones, more and more decisively—understood as systems enabling each individual to give vent to his or her passions, which tends to mean ensuring the freedom to be a slave. One is reminded of Rousseau's paradoxical utterance that we must, in certain cases, compel people to be free.[2] A dreadfully dangerous formula, for it is easy to imagine how this well-meaning constraint could easily take up tyrannical aspects.[3] In any case, our Western, democratic societies are making the very opposite of this authoritarian stance the leading principle of our societies: enabling every individual to live out the kind of life in which he or she offers no resistance to what goads him or her toward any whim whatsoever.

What we mistake for freedom is in such cases a total pliability, a total surrender to what governs us, so that we don't feel any reluctance to yield.

Spinoza already unmasked such a mock freedom by saying that the drunkard thinks he is free to drink, the chatterbox thinks that she is free to gossip, and so on, in the same way as a stone endowed with consciousness would feel free to fall.[4]

Here we have to listen to Kant's stern teaching: being the slave of one's passions, yielding to whatever is in us, is, as he calls it, "pathological," and giving vent to it is hardly freedom, but on the contrary, bondage. The fact that our passions are felt as being inside us, so that they don't count as an external pressure, scarcely makes a difference. According to the German philosopher, only obedience to the moral law enables us to act freely, that is, really to act as ourselves, as the persons who we are.[5] Hence, what is difficult in the program "doing what we want" is the precise nature of the "we" that is supposed to "want."

The task of building one's "I" for freedom can be described with the help of a zoological parable of sorts. A jellyfish is driven by the current and the tides, to which it totally submits because its ability to move is so limited. A shellfish builds around its soft flesh a solid coat of armor, like the sea urchin. It thereby gains safety but gives up any mobility. Fish interiorize the shell and make of it a spine. So do, for that matter, all kinds of higher animals from the reptiles to the mammals. Vertebrates are urchins turned inside out. Their soft parts are outside and can easily fall prey to all kind of predators. But the gain in mobility is overwhelming and enables them to choose among a great many strategies of escape and conquest.

Levels of Freedom

Let me now try to put some order into the rather chaotic idea of freedom by classifying different levels of it or, to be precise, different ways of giving freedom a concrete existence according to the level of the beings to which it accrues. I must here run counter to a common assumption, for, as a rule, freedom is considered as a privilege of rational beings, which means—since the rational beings that we commonly experience are human rather than angelic—as a privilege of man. Some thinkers even interpreted the traditional definition of man—*zōon logon echon* (Greek, "living creature having speech") or *animal rationale* (Latin, "rational animal")—as meaning "the *free* living being." We can trace to its source a thin rivulet of philosophical tradition that emphasizes freedom as the definitional characteristic of the human. It goes through Alexander of Aphrodisias, Gregory of Nyssa, Bernard of Clairvaux, and the Franciscan Pierre de Jean Olieu[6] and came to a head in Jean-Jacques Rousseau,[7] not to mention existentialist authors of the twentieth century.

To be sure, freedom in the fullest meaning of the word exists in spiritual beings only, but it has analogous forms in beings that occupy a lower rung on the scale of life. Language gives us a hint by using words that imply some sort of freedom. We should take seriously those ways of speaking and consider them as more than metaphors. Let me take as my Ariadne's clew not so much the static fact of being free but the dynamic fact of becoming free.

(1) For the most elementary energies, the equivalent of freedom is *liberation*. The energy lying hidden in the nucleus of atoms can be set free with greater or smaller ease. This can be brought about relatively easily in the case of uranium. This has not yet been done for the simple atom of hydrogen. In principle, though, energy lies in the core of any kind of matter. The difference between matter and energy is only superficial. In reality, they are two sides of the same coin. Matter is bound energy.

(2) For the elements, freedom consists in the removal of an obstacle that thwarts a spontaneous tendency. In the case of heavy bodies, like stones or even parachutists before they open their parachute, we speak of a "free" fall. In this sense, we speak in mechanics of the six "degrees of freedom" of solid bodies, meaning thereby the directions in which they can move or rotate.

(3) For plants, it is unimpeded growth, reaching for sunlight and for water, trees spreading their boughs and twigs, plunging their roots deep into the soil, and even bypassing obstacles.

(4) For the more complicated mechanisms involved in the organs of living beings, like glands, it is triggering, *release*, lifting, withdrawal of the inhibition.

(5) For living beings considered as wholes, be they animals that have been trapped by hunters or even human beings caught by slave hunters, it is fleeing from the cage or the jail, *escape* or *deliverance*.

(6) For rational beings, freedom is *choice*. There are stepping-stones in Greek philosophy already, for example for *logos* as freedom in Aristotle with the notion of a "logical power" (*dynamis logikē*), as distinguished from a person "without *logos*" (*aneu logou*). The physician can choose to cure or poison his/her patient. But putting the two ways on the same level is only an abstraction. In fact, something always tips the scales in favor of one horn of the dilemma, what Aristotle calls a "principle of motion" (*archē kinēseōs*) in the soul (*psychē*).[8] Free choice supposes the so-called freedom of indifference.

(7) For slaves, there is an official, legal act that ensures that their freedom won't be menaced anymore, by the name of *freeing*.

(8) For social beings, freedom becomes liberty. The duality of words that mirrors the dual character of the English language, made of Germanic and Romance words, is a useful prop for the distinction to be made between freedom as a moral, and even metaphysical feature of human beings on the one hand and liberty as qualifying the political status of people living under certain social and political systems.

Here we can listen to powerful voices from the past three centuries:

Spinoza: "The true goal of the commonwealth is liberty" (*finis ergo Reipublicae revera libertas est*).

David Hume: "Liberty is the perfection of civil society; but still authority must be acknowledged essential to its very existence."

Lord Acton: "Liberty is not a means to a higher political end; it is itself the highest political end."[9]

The excommunicated Jew, the lapsed Presbyterian, and the devout Catholic express thereby an assumption made possible, in the last analysis, by biblical religion.[10]

The Biblical Idea of a New Beginning

Let me now come back to the Bible. The basic new idea introduced by it is the idea of a radical new beginning. This may at first blush look abstract, far from the narrative character of the Holy Book. In order to lend some weight to my claim, let me mention three examples, three places in which this abstract idea receives a concrete realization. They are interesting for our purpose because they take up and illustrate the highest levels of freedom that I have just been mentioning.

(1) *The first one, which deserves pride of place, is the new beginning* tout court, *the new beginning in being, that is, the idea of creation.* This doesn't necessarily mean a beginning in time, since the church fathers already answered the question by conceiving a creation *with* time, the latter being considered as a property of motion, in Aristotelian or Epicurean style, and motion presupposing the existence of moving bodies.[11] The idea of a creation out of whole cloth (ex nihilo) is not clear in the Hebrew Bible, not even in the Midrash, and it remained unclear in later Jewish philosophy, which kept toying with the idea of a primordial matter that the Creator simply put into order in the sublunary world, not to mention the possible eternity of the heavenly spheres.

(2a) *In the intellectual development of the biblical worldview, the idea of a creation of the whole world probably was gained by reasoning backward from another new beginning, more accessible to human memory, that is, the creation of a people.* This was a liberation wrought by the intervention of a God radically external to the realm of mankind. In the case of Israel, we have the basic biblical narrative of the exodus from Egyptian bondage, a collective freeing which is the first expression of freedom in the Bible. The story may have had a historical basis, probably at a smaller scale than what is told in the book of Exodus. In any case, the Hebrew language may have kept a trace of the way in which the people understood its own identity, since the word for "free man," *ḥofšī*, is said to have meant "slave" in Canaanite.[12]

(2b) *On the level of the individual, a new beginning in human action is realized by freedom as spontaneity and creativity.* The relevance of the idea of a new beginning for freedom was repeatedly pointed out by Hannah Arendt, on the basis of a reading of Augustine that led her to a very felicitous misinterpretation of a passage in *The City of God*: "That there be a beginning, man was created before whom there was nobody" ([initium] ut esset, creatus est homo, ante quem nullus fuit).[13] In the Hebrew Bible, this is set on the stage in the scenes in which a choice is proposed, in a situation that implies a radical new beginning, represented in narrative form as the entering of a yet untrodden country. This happened when the people had to choose its God at the end of the book of Joshua (24:14–15), or more basically, when Israel was summoned to choose between life and death at the end of Deuteronomy (30:19).

(3) *A new beginning in moral life is brought about through forgiveness.* Forgiveness is not a philosophical concept, not a part of moral philosophy, even if the latter is allowed to explore it with its own intellectual tools and may do that successfully.[14] Moral philosophy tells us what we should do and avoid. But once its precepts are not abided by, it has nothing more to tell us, short of repeating the rule. What Greek philosophers meant by *syngnōmē* was a taking into account of human weakness, not mercy properly speaking. Forgiveness is the possibility of starting again. To be sure, this doesn't happen totally from scratch, but at least from a clean slate. In a psalm, David, or whoever the inspired writer might have been, asks God: "Create in me a clean heart" (Ps. 51:10). Interestingly, the verb for "to create," *bara'*, is a rare one, a term of art whose subject can be God only, and which designates creation properly speaking. In the verse, the parallel phrase is "make new [*ḥdš*] in me a firm spirit" (trans. mine).

By this token, we are faced with three ideas—creation, freedom, and forgiveness—that constitute some sort of set of Borromean rings. I wonder whether freedom is, on the one hand, intellectually thinkable without the idea of creation and, on the other hand, livable for average human beings without the idea of forgiveness.

Freedom and Creation

Let us ponder awhile the link between freedom and creation. I will bring out two points.

First, faith in creation makes freedom understandable as freedom for the good. In spite of all possible natural catastrophes and human crimes, the world is the work of a benevolent God, not of the bogey imagined by ancient or modern Gnosticism. Against A. E. Housman's "whatever brute or blackguard made the world," the Creator is neither an incompetent bungler who made a slapdash world nor a cunning sadist who contrived a perfect jail. His final aim is the same as ours. Hence, our striving for the good is not the enterprise of a castaway, alone on a makeshift raft of meaning floating on an ocean of nonsense. It is in keeping with the global tendency of the world, taken at its deepest level and in the teeth of all appearances.[15]

Second, and conversely, the experience of freedom makes faith in creation a meaningful choice. I said "choice," because we are facing two possibilities of what the Latin Scholastics called *aseitas*. Something must exist out of itself—in Latin, *a se*. Either inanimate matter or God has this property. There may be a bevy of good reasons for us to choose the latter candidate for *aseitas*, that is, God. In any case, this choice has two consequences:

(a) *If we think of God on the analogy of a rational being, creation will become less opaque and unintelligible.* We will find in ourselves an equivalent of the creative act whose presence we suppose in him. This equivalent is our ability to initiate a series of causes by a decision of our freedom. Freedom is the equivalent in man of the idea of a creation by God. Each and every free act is some sort of creation on a smaller scale. This makes the idea of creation somehow—namely, analogically—understandable.[16]

(b) *We can become the dialogue partners of a rational Being.* His will underlies the whole show. Not a blind desire, not a whim, but a benevolent, reasonable will, suffused with wisdom and *logos*, that has put us and, together with us, whatever led to our being, from the remotest galaxy to our parents, into being out of sheer love. We will be, literally, on speaking terms with God. Prayer will become a meaningful enterprise, and together with it intellectual inquiry into the logic underlying an intelligible world, that is, science.

Creation and Forgiveness

The claim of the Bible is that God created a world which is basically, and in its whole, "very good." This is the teaching of the first narrative about creation (Gen. 1:31). As a consequence, this means that whatever is wrong in the world does not originate in a flaw in the structure of created beings, let alone in the presence of "two powers in Heaven," to quote the traditional Jewish formula for the Manichaean outlook. Evil must have arisen at some later time. There are few happier news items than "shit happens," for this means that "shit" is not essential, but accidental. What happened can go. How it happened is precisely what the second biblical narrative about the origin tells us (Gen. 3). By this token, the burden of responsibility lies on the shoulders of some created beings—and in particular on ours, too, as we must do good and avoid evil. Hence, we badly need to be forgiven. Freedom is something that enables us to require and receive forgiveness.

It is in such a context that we experience our freedom. We discover it when we realize that it is lame, that we are unable not only to *do* what we want but *really to want* what we want. We should not take for granted that we are still able to reach the Good and, first of all, to want it—that is, to want it not only by making a vain wish but by doing whatever is required for us to get what we want. The basic Christian experience is that we don't do what we want and don't want what we do. From the point of view of the historian of ideas, this is a new idea that arose in Augustine.[17] But the Latin father's emphasis on the weakness of the will moves in the wake of Paul's sigh: "To will is present with me; but how to perform that which is good I find not" (Rom. 7:14–25; quotation from v. 18, trans. mine). There is some foretaste of this experience among pagans and Jews as well: among pagans like Ovid, Seneca, and Epictetus and, among Jews, in a text from the Qumran library.[18] On the other hand, there is no clear concept of freedom of the will in pre-Christian antiquity. The words that we translate with "freedom"—the Greek *eleutheria*, the Latin *libertas*, and, for that matter, the Hebrew *herūt* and, later on, the Arabic *hurriya*—all designate the social status of whoever is not a slave, and nothing more.[19]

This new Christian view of freedom is somehow complex. A simpler religion like Islam insists on man being the slave of God. In common Arabic parlance, human beings are called "the slaves" (*al-ʿibād*). Furthermore, the aim of the law, or at least of some of its commandments, is said by some legal scholars to be "the mere enslavement" (*taʿabbud maḥḍ*) of man.[20] To be sure, God's mercy is harped upon in the Islamic sources and repeatedly recalled to the mind of the pious in Islamic everyday life. But this mercy simply consists in God's will not to take into account sins and to wash away the stains left by them. The original nature of man (*fitra*)— which, by the way, is supposed to be essentially and eternally submitted to God, in Arabic *muslim* (Qur'an 7:172)—remains unspoiled by them.

Christianity is more complicated. It takes human freedom seriously. It takes sin—that is, the implicit decision of human beings to live away from God—with the utmost seriousness and respects it. Therefore, it is somehow pessimistic, since it admits that human freedom was wounded so that it has lost its ability to do the good that it acknowledges and approves of, and even dreams of; that freedom is now too weak really to desire, let alone to bring about, that good. Therefore, the God of the Christians had to mount a tricky operation—what theologians call the "economy of salvation"—for man to become able to cure his lame freedom.

Now, we are still left without any precise doctrine of freedom. My claim is that a full understanding of what freedom is all about has to retrieve the totality of the models of freedom that occur in earlier, more primitive stages of being than political liberty. I already pointed out the presence of the highest of those stages in the biblical experience.[21] Let me here round out the picture by taking two examples from the realm of the prehuman. I hope to let you see that some of these low realizations of what will come to a special flourishing in human beings can help us better understand what this flourishing consists in.

Freedom as Free Growth

The free growth of the plant confronts us with a very interesting paradox. I will spend some time with it, because it will help us understand other, higher forms of freedom. Plants are made of substances that are earthly or watery (modern scientists would say solid and liquid). As such, they are heavy in nature. A clod of earth falls down, and water flows from the source toward the sea. Nevertheless, plants develop in the upward direction. They plunge their roots in the depth so that they might be able to draw the nourishing stuffs from earthly moisture, but also for them to get a firm footing so that they may be able to rise higher and higher toward the sun. This growth is combined with, and even presupposes, an ability to resist the spontaneous tendency of heavy bodies to reach for the lowest possible place. This tendency is still there in the plant: as soon as the parts are separated from the whole, they follow their natural tendency and fall. A twig that we chop off falls down, a leaf torn off by a gust of wind falls down, a ripe apple falls down, even if Isaac Newton is not underneath.

This is not the same thing as choosing the whole over against the part, which is a common phenomenon, beginning perhaps from the so-called apoptosis of cells and ending with the sacrifice of an animal on behalf of its offspring or of the warrior in favor of the country, and so on. This happens in the category of quantity, where a simple reckoning is enough, so that it is relatively easy to choose—at least seen from the outside, from the point of view of the high priest Caiaphas (John 11:50). But here, on the other hand, the entities pitted against each other are not a part and the whole to which it belongs, but two views of the same whole. There is an inferior way to look at the tree and a superior one. The former sees it as wood or even as timber; the latter perceives in it life.

Now, what is free growth for the tree is constraint for each and every part of the wood which it consists of. Freedom already appears as a way for things to resist the spontaneous tendencies of the elements they are made of. The case of vegetative growth shows us that we may have to downplay, or even sacrifice, some dimensions of our own being in order to become what we really are.

Freedom as Free Access to the Good

My second example is the humblest phenomenon in whose case we use the adjective "free," that is, "free fall." It has something to teach us about our own freedom. This was seen most clearly by Augustine, who has taken up the image and lifted it up to the dignity of a philosophical thought in his famous "my weight is my love" (*pondus meum amor meus*).[22] This presupposed a theory of gravity that is now outdated. Modern, post-Galilean physics has replaced it by the writing of mathematical laws. Yet this view fitted well with our everyday experience on the surface of the Earth.

In any case, it may still make sense, not as a description of physical reality, but as a basic metaphor. Well now, according to this theory, elementary bodies look for their natural place. The heavy ones, like a stone or a lump of metal, strive toward the center of the earth, whereas light ones, like fire (which used to be considered as a simple element), go upward. This is so because they want to get to where they are fully what they are—in Aristotle's technical vocabulary, where they reach their "entelechy," their perfect fulfillment. They in a sense "walk" toward their entelechy (*badizein eis entelecheian*) in the same way as whatever is in potency is said to "walk" toward its actuality.[23] By so doing, they reach their own good.

I insist on the adjective "their own." Heaven forfend that freedom should consist in yielding to external duress or interiorized temptation. Freedom is the unfolding of what we really and essentially are, in the core of our being. Now, getting to this core is not an easy task, but, on the contrary, requires a great deal of work.

Here we possibly could do justice to a basic intuition of the French philosopher Henri Bergson: a free act is something rare; for the most part we move along the old ruts and do what we are accustomed to do. "We are free when our acts emanate from the whole of our personality, when they express it, when they have that indefinable likeness to it which we sometimes observe between the work and the artist."[24]

The most common view of freedom as realizing itself in choice is not sufficient. Real freedom is a choice that arises from the whole of our being, not from a faculty that could weigh two possibilities against one another and tip the scales in favor of one of them. The model of the two ways to be taken pervades Western thought from the Greeks—with Hesiod or the sophist Prodikos—to Robert Frost.[25] It leaves us faced with the predicament so well expressed by Yogi Berra: "When you come to a fork in the road, take it." Having to choose is not the purest form of freedom. There is a recurrent temptation to bestow on the "bad" possibility the same dignity as on the "good" one. Still worse is the idea that experiencing evil could enable us better to know the good and more decidedly to choose it.[26] In fact, the evil blinds us to its own character.

Freedom is what enables us to reach the Good. Dante has a wonderful image, at the same time poetically beautiful and philosophically balanced: We are like caterpillars; we were born so that we might build in us the angelic butterfly which escapes its chrysalis and flies upward, toward Justice without screens. The butterfly has to get rid of its cocoon, but this is a necessary, not a sufficient, condition. It still has to ply its wings in order to soar upward:

Non v'accorgete voi, che noi siam vermi,
Nati a formar l'angelica farfalla,
Che vola alla giustizia senza schermi?[27]

Are you not aware that we are worms, born to form the angelic butterfly that flies unto judgment without defenses?

CHAPTER SIX

Culture as a By-Product

What we free people do in the world and what we make out of what we find in it—what we find being nature—could be summed up under the heading of "culture." In order to shed some light on this highly obscure notion, I found no better way than to take my bearings from a lecture Pope Benedict gave on this topic in Paris on September 12, 2008. I had the privilege of attending. The elite of the Parisian intelligentsia was there, and its predicament was huge. To judge by the puzzled expression of their faces, those big shots obviously could not make heads or tails of it. What was the pope driving at? What was the upshot of this meditation on monkish life in the Middle Ages, that is, on a walk of life which is not ours and which, moreover, belonged to a historical period that is not ours and has been, for many of us, given good riddance to?

I must confess that my humble self in person understood only a little bit of what the pope was telling us. I had to read the text of his lecture more than once.[1] Let me now endeavor better to take advantage of Benedict's insights.

Culture as Superfluous

I will take my bearings from a working definition of culture. It badly needs refining. Culture is the set of the answers to the basic questions of mankind, be they humdrum or lofty: Whom shall I marry? What shall I eat and how shall I cook my meals? How shall I behave with my social and natural surrounding? Whom shall I worship? In each case, a culture distinguishes a right and a wrong behavior, hence what we call "values." What we call a culture or a civilization is a definite set of answers that distinguish a right way and a wrong one: thou shalt marry a suitable person belonging to this group, and not have incestuous commerce; thou shalt eat this food and not that disgusting filth; thou shalt worship this god of ours and not that foreign idol, and so on.

Moreover, we must distinguish two sets of elements in which we tell our right way from the wrong way of the others. Some deal with the very foundations of human life: the life of the individual, with food, clothing, and so on, or the survival of the group with marriage and education. Now, "culture" in this meaning is hardly common parlance; it is rather a high-flown term of art used by anthropologists. There is in culture something else, which is not strictly necessary, and this is for the most part what we common people usually call by the name of "culture," for instance art, religion, philosophy, and science. Let us call this "higher culture." Aristotle makes an important point about this kind of culture, for which he chooses, for obvious reasons, the example of philosophical pursuits, summarized in the searching for causes. He observes that such an endeavor can arise only after basic needs have been met by various arts. He further points out that it requires a leisure class, and he gives as an example the priests in Egypt, who had nothing very much to do, apart, as a matter of course, from the ritual deeds that were their job.[2]

What the Greek philosopher tells us from Athens was taught in Jerusalem, too. Let me now look at the Bible and read a satire on the origin of idolatry which is to be found in the second part of the book of the prophet Isaiah (44:9–20). This passage is meant as lampooning idolatry, as poking fun at the stupidity of people who adore dumb and powerless statues of wood and stone. The theme is a hackneyed one in Jewish, Christian, and Muslim apologists. It is even trite in so-called pagan authors, like the Latin poet Horace, who, unlike Isaiah in the bitter mood of this passage, contents himself with an indulgent smile.[3]

In Isaiah, the sculptor had first cooked his meal and warmed himself with the wood a part of which he is about to sculpt into a god. The prophet has the idol-monger say: "Oh! I warm myself and I look at the flame" (44:16b, trans. mine). The sentence is, at first sight, rather redundant and could very well be overlooked. Yet it expresses two important ideas: the first one is reflexivity, knowing what one does. The second idea is the aesthetic moment. Fire is not only a way for us to warm our bodies or to roast meat and boil vegetables. It has a beauty of its own. We can spend long hours of daydreaming while contemplating the burning logs of an open fire in a chimney.

A very important word is uttered by the author of the biblical satire on idolatry that I have quoted. The idol is made out of what is left (*še'ērīṯ*) of the wood (44:17a). Culture is basically "superfluous," a word that is more often than not taken with a derogatory shade of meaning. Yet its etymology teaches us something important: culture is, literally, *overflowing*. This is the first sense in which I claim that culture is a by-product.

The Aesthetic Sense

Human beings can get interested in things that are not useful, for their own sake. We need not look at the flame in order to feel its warmth. This property we find in some things we call "beauty." In beauty, two meanings of "interest" clash against each other. Interest can designate what pays off, like the interests of a loan. But we know that what is interesting can exist beyond, or even in the teeth of, what is useful for us. This is, by the way, the classical definition of the beautiful by Kant.[4]

Beauty is lovable, but the love of beauty is of a special kind: it doesn't aim at getting its object, but keeps the distance that enables enjoying by contemplating. This is nicely captured by the word "amateur," from *amare*, "to love," but with the shade of meaning of some detachment. Now, being an amateur is a specifically human feature. To quote C. S. Lewis: "Man is the only amateur animal; all the others are professionals. They have no leisure and do not desire it. When God made the beasts dumb He saved the world from infinite boredom, for if they could speak they would all of them, all day, talk nothing but shop."[5]

This presence of an aesthetic sense among prehistoric human beings as soon as one and a half million years before Christ receives a powerful confirmation from recent discoveries of paleontologists.[6] They report the discovery in some prehistoric tombs of some weird artifacts, like primitive axes or knives, the so-called bifaces, or simply spheres made of a beautiful kind of flint, chert, or basalt, polished with great care. Those objects were very carefully wrought, that is, at the cost of many hours of labor, but they never were used for a practical purpose. On the cutting edge of the bifaces, there is no trace of use, and no tear and wear on the surface of those perfect spheres. This means that they never were used, but put along corpses in tombs, probably as offerings fraught with a symbolic meaning. They may have had a cultic purpose, as a gift of sorts to the deceased, but this is anybody's guess.

To sum up, this "superfluous" dimension of culture was highlighted by the Greeks as well as by ancient Israel. The two cultures concur in a common matter, even if they express it in different styles, conceptual for the Greeks, narrative for the Jews.

Now, this feature, being a by-product, holds good for culture in general. What about Christian culture? The question deserves to be asked all the more since this Christian culture is often described as blending Greek and Jewish elements, as hailing both from Athens and Jerusalem, either taking after both or building a fruitful tension between those two poles. Let us now look at this specific case and, to begin with, at the example chosen by Pope Benedict.

Salvaging Ancient Culture

The example he puts at the center of his meditation is, as I observed at the outset, rather surprising: monastic life in the Middle Ages. According to Pope Benedict, the intention of the medieval monks was definitely not to create culture, not even to preserve an earlier culture. Now, it is the case that they splendidly achieved what they didn't want. Historically speaking, too, their cultural doings were by-products. Benedict is eager to remind his hearers of this fact and feat, but he simply mentions it *en passant*, as a side issue.[7]

Let me briefly expand his allusion. Monks succeeded in preserving the legacy of classical Latin literature. This happened in troubled times, when the very survival of ancient culture in the Latin West was at stake. A watershed is the death of Boethius, in 524, five years before the events that led to the closure of the philosophical (Platonic) School of Athens by the emperor Justinian. Boethius, a patrician of old stock, was among the very few Romans who had kept a good knowledge of Greek. Now, precisely because of the ebb of Greek knowledge in the West, he felt the need for a translation of the Greek philosophers of the Socratic tradition. He therefore endeavored to translate Plato and Aristotle and to comment upon both of them. He could not fulfill his vast project, for, accused of a secret correspondence with the emperors of Constantinople, who already were planning to conquer again the Western part of the empire, he was thrown into jail, where he wrote his masterpiece, the *Consolation of Philosophy*, and was put to death.

Boethius was not a monk. One generation later, however, in 555, another Roman nobleman, Cassiodorus, attempted something along very much the same lines when he founded in Calabria—that is, the last tip of the Italian Peninsula, the toes of the riding boot—the convent of Vivarium, whose exact location is still unknown to the archaeologists. This convent had as its essential part a large library, together with a scriptorium in which manuscripts were not only kept and read but copied, hence preserved for posterity.[8] Interestingly, Cassiodorus very consciously imitated the convent of Nisibis, at the northern border of present-day Iraq, a convent which harbored also a school, in which the language of teaching was Syriac.[9]

The whole network of Benedictine abbeys, which spread all over Western Europe, was instrumental in our still having Latin literature at our disposal even though the Western Roman Empire vanished. In a word, monks hardly contented themselves with singing vespers in the Temple of Jupiter amidst the ruins of the Capitol in front of Edward Gibbon.[10] They were powerfully and efficiently instrumental in helping ancient culture over the gap that had opened between the ancient world and what was to become the so-called Middle Ages.

What is especially interesting is that those monks did not throw a buoy to, or build a raft for, Christian literary castaways only. The bulk of what they helped climb on board was pagan literature. Among pagan authors, some, to be sure, could be kind of baptized post mortem. Vergil could be read as a prophet of sorts because of the long misinterpretation of the 4th Eclogue, and Seneca was believed to have had a correspondence with Saint Paul, and so on. But why did the monks keep the historians, or the bawdy Catullus, or the lewd Ovid, let alone Lucretius the Epicurean atheist?

All this was made possible by what I called elsewhere the Pauline revolution.[11] It drew a wedge between paganism and Judaism, which both were cultures as well as religions. On the one hand, Greek *paideia* was a package deal of sorts. It included what we would call highbrow literacy, such as appears in the epics by Homer. It included, too, sport at the palestra. Last and certainly not least, it included sacrifices to the civic gods. Tragedy arose as part and parcel of the feasts of the god Dionysus. Even the philosophers organized themselves as cult-guilds. To the places in which we keep what we consider to be precious we still give the name "museums," which means temples of the Muses. Roman education stressed military prowess and evolved into a cult of the emperor as embodying the legitimacy of Roman rule over the Mediterranean. On the other hand, Jewish scholars already planned to extract from the Torah a whole system of rules, the "way of life," in Hebrew *halakha*. In principle, like the later Islamic *shari'a*, it was meant to provide ready answers to any question about what is to be done in any situation.

By this token, pagans as well as Jews had full-fledged systems of culture, embedded in a religion. Now Paul brought about a sea change. He severed culture from religion, over against the Greek *paideia* and the Jewish halakha. The Torah had to undergo a severe slimming cure. Of the 613 commandments that it contains, Paul kept only the Decalogue in its literal sense and interpreted the other ones as allegories. Now, the halakha was supposed to answer whatever question could be asked on how to behave in all the circumstances of daily life. As a consequence, faced with the problem of the good life, the Christian believer was left empty-handed, barring some very general moral principles. He had to look elsewhere for precise guidelines. This "elsewhere" was found in many places: to begin with, the Roman polity, together with the law that regulated it, and Greek philosophy were drawn upon. But both had lost their religious underpinnings. Pagan culture became only what we call today "culture." It entered a Christian framework, without losing its specificity. In my vocabulary: it was not digested, but included.[12]

When Christianity entered the scene of the ancient world, the content of the framework was what happened to be available on the market of ancient, Greco-Roman, civilization. But the same framework could very well be filled by other contents. Later on, Germanic and Slavic mores, Celtic legends, Arabic and Persian lore and science, entered the melting pot. The Jesuit missionaries didn't object to letting Chinese mores into it in the seventeenth century, but their attempt, as is well known, regrettably failed. In the future, this failure might prove to have been only provisional.

We meet here a paradox: Christian culture is not made of Christian elements.

Culture Not Meant to Be Such

Let us come back to the observation made by Pope Benedict: the monks never dreamed of doing something cultural, let alone of building a Christian culture or civilization. Some may even have thought that their doings and the works of their making were doomed to disappear in a more or less near future. But this didn't prevent them from busying themselves with preservation or furtherance of cultural goods and even with innovation.

A good example is Pope Gregory the Great (540–604). He laid the foundations for the whole Middle Ages, not so much because of the Gregorian chant which was named after him, in both meanings of the phrase. But rather as the harbinger of important reforms in church life, as the last of the four fathers of the Latin church, and as the author of a long commentary on the book of Job, the first comprehensive treatise on morals written by a Christian. Now, people were convinced that the end was at hand, and he shared this feeling. He was sure to be the last pope, or the last but one. He simply wanted to put things away, in the same way as we clean up our house, sweep the carpets, water the plants, feed the goldfish, and so on before leaving for a weekend.

To some extent, the monks were no exception. They were rather the heirs to a millennia-long tradition that hails back to pre-Christian times. For the most part, the objects which our museums are full of were not meant to hang somewhere on the walls of a museum or to lie in a show window. They were meant either to lighten the burden of mankind or to please the gods. Yet the monks who salvaged ancient culture might have been more or less clearly conscious of a fact: there exists between Christianity and culture a link at the same time paradoxical and powerful. It can be described as a mutual need. Mutual, but not symmetric. On the one hand, Christianity needs, as its content, culture, and a culture that it need not produce directly. On the other hand, culture needs Christianity as its ground. In what follows, I will develop these two points.

We remember the paradox: Christian culture is not made of "Christian" elements. Now, it is the flip side of another surprising fact: Christianity never claimed to produce a full-fledged culture. Huge chunks of human experience are left outside of the pale and entrusted to human intelligence—created, to be sure, by divine grace, but unaided by a special revelation. This distinguishes Christianity from other religions. For instance, there is in Judaism a Talmudic cuisine, based on the rules of Kashrut; there are Christian cooks, but there is no Christian cuisine. There is in Islam a so-called prophetic medicine, based on the pieces of advice given by Muhammad in some cases and summarized in some collections of *hadith* which have this name, prophetic medicine;[13] there are Christian physicians, but there is no Christian medicine. There is in Islam an Islamic dress code, the Islamic veil for each grown-up female, the commandment that each adult male let his beard grow and trim his mustache; there are Christian tailors and hairdressers, but there is no Christian fashion.

In a nutshell, there is no such thing as a "specifically" Christian behavior, no desire on the side of Christians to live their concrete, everyday lives apart from other people. This is already what is pointed out in a remarkable early document of Christian apologetic literature, the famous, albeit anonymous, *To Diognetus*. This work probably hails back to the end of the second century, shortly before 200. Christians don't distinguish themselves from other people by a special abode, by a special language, by a special attire or a special diet.[14] This has taken a fresh actuality since our Western countries have been confronted with a militant Islam for which clothes and food have a religious dimension. There shouldn't be, either, any intellectual yearning to claim some "specificity" for cultural achievements.

More important and perhaps more provocative and difficult to swallow, there are no Christian morals, contrary to a common way of speaking. There is a common morality, what C. S. Lewis called the Tao or the "great platitudes," and a Christian understanding of it. Too many people imagine that Christian mores can be put on the same level as folklore. Quaint foreign people have quaint ways, so charming, so interesting for tourists who see them from the outside. As such, they can be tolerated in the private realm, but nothing more. You may wear a kilt if you happen to be a Scotsman, you may eat frogs if you happen to be a Frenchman, you may refrain from killing the unborn in the womb of their mother if you happen to be a Christian, but . . .

The Ten Commandments are a particularly successful summary of this common morality. They are hardly more than a reminder of the natural law that we should not have forgotten, were it not for the original sin and its aftermath in history. This, at least, is the doctrine of Thomas Aquinas, and it remained common knowledge for centuries. Pascal, for example, mentions this doctrine in giving the example of the prohibition of murder: the gospel confirmed the law—that is, the Torah—and the Decalogue only renewed what human beings had received from God before Moses in the person of Noah, to whom each and every human being was to be born.[15]

Culture as Praise

Let us get back to the monks. Since they never considered that their task was "cultural" in nature, what exactly did they do? The answer is obvious, and Pope Benedict reminds us of what is well known but not always understood in its depth: monks worked and prayed. The emphasis on work was grounded on a positive view of labor, hence of the material world, including the body and its humblest needs. This stemmed from a vision of the world as created by a good God, hence as basically good.[16] Let me develop the other aspect, that is, prayer, in the same light.

Prayer is not only asking. It is praise, especially in the Psalms. Now, praising is the necessary consequence, hence the symptom, of a complete immersion in joy. To quote once again C. S. Lewis: "Fully to enjoy is to glorify."[17] We have here another kind of overflowing, which is very much in keeping with the former one which I alluded to, namely the overflowing of human creative activity which is the positive flip side of its superfluity. Praise, in turn, has very much to do with culture. It used to be a basic dimension of poetry. There was in ancient literary theory a genre, by the name of "epainetic," from the Greek *epainos*, which means exactly "praise." The leading figure in this genre was Pindar. Now, some literary scholars of the ancient world went so far as to characterize poetry as essentially "panegyric," that is, as laudatory, even if it doesn't celebrate anybody or anything particular.[18] Perhaps we could venture a step further and claim that praise is the nourishing milieu of art *tout court*, and of culture. You can hardly, say, paint something, be it a landscape, a portrait, or whatnot, without an implicit avowal of the fact that it is good that there should be this landscape or this person for you to paint them. You can scarcely write a story without the basic assumption that it is interesting, even if you'll have to tell most unpleasant things.

Now, we may in a sense examine the conscience of our civilization and ask ourselves: Are we still able to praise? Are we still conscious of possessing something to praise, to thank for? Do we still have access to somebody to whom we could be thankful? What does culture become without the Praiseworthy? Can what is "worth" (that is, the so-called values) be still worthwhile without a metaphysical ground?

The German literary scholar Hugo Friedrich (d. 1978) made the following observation about the Romantic movement: "For the life-culture of the ancient world, as well as for the ages that followed it till the eighteenth century, the top psychological value was joy. It was the value which showed that the wise man or the believer, the knight, the courtier, the learned man of the social elite was about to attain perfection. Sadness, whenever it was not a fleeting state of mind, was considered as a negative value, and for the theologians it was a sin."[19] Romanticism, or at least some aspects of the momentous, all-European Romantic movement, turned all this back to front: joy and serenity left the stage, were frowned upon as commonplace, not to say ridiculously *bourgeois*, and were replaced by melancholy and angst. The old sin of *akedia*, the "noonday devil" who assaults the monk when the heat in his cell becomes unbearable, so that he would dream of forsaking his vocation, received a positive valuation. Intellectual honesty, which faces the ugliness of reality, displaced the love of truth and became, to quote Nietzsche, "our last virtue."[20]

In other words, and in words that play on each other: Can *culture* survive where *cult* has no other object than the ego him/herself? "The cult of the ego" was the title of a trilogy of novels by the late-nineteenth- and early-twentieth-century French writer Maurice Barrès.[21] This cult has swollen into an epidemic ever since, under several names: personal development, self-fulfillment, wellness, and pursuits of that ilk.

Pope Benedict is eager to point out that creativity is not enough.[22] In order to substantiate this claim, let us look at what happens when the only aim of culture is "expressing oneself," as we frequently hear. If this is the case, we need not ask whether there really is something inside of us that deserves to be drawn out and shown to the audience. Anything goes. Montaigne, in a fit of what most probably was the literary cliché of the author's modesty, once spoke of his *Essais* as the excretions of his old age (*des excréments d'un vieil esprit*).[23] An Italian, Piero Manzoni (1933–63), had the pluck to answer my question with great clarity by shifting from the metaphorical to the concrete. In May 1961, he defecated into ninety tin cans, sealed them (thank Goodness!), and sold them under the title of "Artist's Shit." The market price for each of those cans is now around $30,000. Be Manzoni's intentions what they may have been, the fact exposed the absurdity of the idea of the artist's self-expression.

If the alleged human "creativity" is not enough, then, if there should be culture, something like an implicit faith in God's *creation* is required. This will be the last idea that I can elicit from Pope Benedict's speech.

Culture of Being

Pope Benedict especially emphasizes song and music in monastic liturgy. First, to be sure, because of his own gift for and interest in music. But there is far more to it than mere personal taste. In the speech which I am now commenting upon, there is in the original German a passage, a matter of one half page, which was not pronounced in French.[24] It is indeed a side issue: Saint Bernard, or the unknown author of the treatise *De cantu* (On singing), which is commonly ascribed to him, implicitly assimilates singing out of tune to a fall in the "place of dissimilitude," the Platonic-Augustinian *regio dissimilitudinis*, interpreted as the loss of the divine resemblance in which Adam was created.[25] On the occasion of this digression, Benedict drops this rather weird sentence: "The culture of singing is also a *culture of being*" (Die Kultur des Singens [ist] auch *Kultur des Seins*).[26] At first sight, the phrase is puzzling and sounds like a tautology. How could a culture be something else than a culture of being? What would a culture of nothingness look like? This reminds us of another phrase, one by Pope Benedict's friend and predecessor on the papal throne, Saint John Paul II, namely "culture of death."[27] Again, one should ask whether every culture has not to be a culture of life.

In the German-speaking world, some authors already had pitted the "culture of being" against other possible forms of culture: of having, of knowing (H. von Keyserling), of making. In such an outlook, culture is understood as what man does, and whatever is meant by "being" or the other notions that are set up against it is only a dimension of the human. The question is whether human beings should *have* something, *know* something, *make* something, or simply "become what they are." This may make a great deal of sense.

Yet let me here take "being" seriously, that is, in its broadest scope, and capitalize it. In the present case, we may ask: What has singing, as an example of culture at large, to do with something like ontology as its underpinning? What does ontology teach us on what culture is all about? Or, to put it the other way, what does culture teach us about Being, about what sort of thing Being must be or, better, *how* Being must be for it to have something to do with culture? What must be its relationship to culture? Is Being the aim and object of a culture? Or rather its origin and ground, its nourishing soil? You'll have guessed that the latter is my hunch.

Singing is celebrating, praising. Now, obviously, we can sing, hence praise, only what is good. We can move in the element of praise, which is the condition of culture, if and only if there is something praiseworthy. In the last analysis, there can be culture if and only if we are convinced that, in the teeth of whatever evil is rampant, being is intrinsically good. Which is kind of an ontological choice. This choice is presupposed in any culture-grounding activity. Our task doesn't consist only in producing cultural goods. This is a necessary and highly recommendable activity with which I have no quarrel. At a deeper level, however, our task consists in making culture possible in the first place. And we do that by asserting the goodness of what is, by confessing something like our faith in Being. This is the last, basic sense in which culture is a by-product.

Values or Virtues?

When I am in a gloomy mood, which happens from time to time, I wonder whether it would not have made more sense for me to spare the time I spent writing a book on European cultural identity and, later, doing research on related issues. I could have devoted this time to other intellectual pursuits. Among the first objects of a possible study that spring to my mind are languages of the ancient Middle East such as Egyptian or Akkadian. The beauty of the cultures that expressed themselves in those languages is that there is no doubt about their being dead as doornails. Whether European culture is still alive is a moot question. It sometimes gives the impression that it is some sort of a zombie, a corpse that keeps walking. My fellow countryman Jacques Delors, then president of the European Commission, is commonly believed to have, in 1992, coined the formula, widely echoed afterward, that we should give back to Europe a soul. Which implies that it has lost it, that is, that it is at present literally inanimate. Many people translate this plea into the vocabulary of "values" which is now rampant whenever politicians or, for that matter, opinion makers of all ilks try to legitimate their doings.

The Value of Values

This prompts me to give a bit of thought to the very idea of a value and of what a value is all about. I certainly won't plead against European values. Heaven forbid that I should even think of doing that. But I would advocate some more caution in our preaching on their behalf, more precisely on our calling them by the name of values.

Describing what European values are would not give us much mileage, and praising them would amount to bringing coal to Newcastle. Things like the rule of law; fair opportunities for everybody, male or female; mass education; cheap copies of masterpieces of painting or music; and freedom, and in particular freedom of scientific research, are commonly agreed upon, at least in European countries. Whether they are actually enforced is another kettle of fish. What is important is the kind of behavior that the care for such values induces, or should induce, in the European mind. Concrete respect for the freedom of other people and law-abiding behavior are more important than principles.

On the other hand, we should ask why all those good things, those things whose goodness can hardly be gainsaid, receive the name of "values," a word that might be not that harmless, not as harmless, anyway, as is commonly assumed. Let us perform what filmmakers call a "dollying out" and move the camera backward. Let us ask how the kind of behavior that answers the call of values was understood in the past. Not just any past state of civilization, but the past that gave birth to European culture.

The first surprise that awaits us is that we don't have to go that far backward to watch the disappearance of the concept of "value." For it is not very ancient. To be sure, ancient civilizations were aware of the market price of wares. And the Stoics spoke of the *axia* of goods, what literally tips the scales (*agein*) in favor of a good. In modern times, the idea was taken over, under the name of "price," by people like Montaigne and Pascal. It had a career in political economy. In both contexts, it meant the worth *of* somebody (his or her courage, in the first place) or of something. But the idea of "the values" became common parlance only after it had been powerfully orchestrated by Nietzsche in the late nineteenth century, and one generation later by the German phenomenological philosopher Max Scheler, although he hardly pulled his punches against his older fellow countryman.[1]

The Virtue of Virtues

It is a matter of common knowledge that the main sources of European higher culture are to be found in classical antiquity and in the Bible. To use a pair of rather hackneyed catchwords, they arose in "Athens" as well as in "Jerusalem." Now, those two sources agreed for the most part on the content of what is right and what is wrong. But they interpreted what is good or evil in different ways. Let me insist on this point: there are no such things as morals with an epithet. There are no "pagan" or "Jewish," "Islamic" or "Buddhist" morals, nor for that matter a "humanist" morals, and for heaven's sake no "Christian" morals. There undoubtedly are, on the other hand, different ways to understand what moral behavior is all about: doing good and avoiding evil may be a way for me to make lighter the karma of my deeds and climb a rung on the ladder of reincarnations; it may be a way to obey God's commandments, thereby deserving paradise; it may be a way to stick to the *bushido* of the samurai, to the code of honor of the gentleman, or of the "*pukka sahib* who plays the game and doesn't do things that are not done";[2] it may be a way for me to do my act of kindness; and so on. But as for what is concretely to be done, there are not that many ways to help an old lady across a street . . .

As for the most commonly accepted outlooks that molded our Western world, let us choose as spokesmen for the "Athenian" one the philosophers, Greek or Roman. All call what prompts us to do good "virtues." Now, the Greek word for "virtue," *aretē*, can designate the excellence of any kind of being, not only human beings. For instance, it made sense for the Greeks to speak of the "virtue" of a horse, that is, its swiftness in running. Plato's Socrates begins by asking what the virtue of a horse is and then shifts to the trickier case of human virtues.[3] Our European languages kept this meaning till a relatively recent time, when they spoke of the curative virtue of a plant or of a gem. In the seventeenth century, this was already beginning to become obsolete, wherefore Molière poked fun of the alleged *virtus dormitiva* of opium.[4]

Now, running is a natural property of the horse; its ability to run faster than other ones is the peak of this natural endowment. Human care can help such beings to attain their perfection: a colt must be properly broken and groomed for it to become a good charger. Virtues are grounded in the nature of things. For us human beings, "doing good" means that we bring to fulfillment what is human in us, what constitutes the deepest core of our humanity. We do that by bringing out what most decidedly expresses what kind of beings we are, that is, rational beings, for rationality is our nature.

As for the Hebrew Bible, it doesn't possess a word for nature, although the idea can undergird many narratives.[5] The actions that it praises are very much the same as what the Greeks deemed praiseworthy. But it calls them by another name, that is, "commandments." In the Bible, rulings that make possible justice and charity are issued by a transcendent Being whom biblical writers call by the name of God. This God reveals himself in the course of history and as the one who shapes history (Isa. 44:24–28). This God issued orders as clauses of a covenant with mankind at large (Gen. 9:9), and later on with Israel as God's chosen people (Exod. 19:5). "Doing good and avoiding evil" means that one abides by God's commandments. In present-day Jewish parlance, any good deed is still commonly called a *mitzvah*, that is, literally a "commandment." Human perfection is lawfulness as listening to God's voice.

Values as a Go-Between

We modern people prefer to speak of values. Now, this can be understood as a means to steer a middle course between the ancient and the biblical outlooks. I would rather say that this is a way of playing the one against the other. Modern thought as a whole often tries to get rid of both worldviews and to drive a wedge of its own between them by using the one as a weapon against the other, criticizing paganism with moral tools biblical in origin and the Bible with ancient, pagan intellectual implements.[6] The question that remains is whether this synthesis is stable, hence, long-lived, rather than the fly of one day.

In particular, the utterly modern notion of "values" borrows some elements from both premodern sources of our culture. From the biblical view, they get some dimension of transcendence. Values are above us, they are the target of our striving, what we are driving at, perhaps as a goal that can't be reached, but are the object of an indefinite yearning or, to speak like the German philosopher Fichte, a "striving" (*Streben*).[7] From the ancient, classical—"pagan" if we want—outlook, values borrow their immanent dimension. They are not divine in origin, but human.

In both cases, however, the modern outlook turns against its sources. Such a turn affects the ground of moral obligation. Over against the Bible, it rejects the grounding of the good on God's will and wisdom. And over against classical Greek and Roman philosophy, it rejects its grounding on any natural properties of beings. The English philosopher

G. E. R. Moore has pushed this dismissal of any grounding to its logical consequences in his critique of what he calls the "naturalistic fallacy," a mistake in which the divine unexpectedly appears as being as "natural" as, say, the interests.[8]

The only available ground for action must be our freedom. We are supposed to be free, autonomous beings that need not be driven to action by any external principle, including this paradoxical *inside outsider* which we call our "nature." Modern man is supposed neither to hearken to any divine being over above him, nor to have any nature, but to decide freely what he/she will do, and even what he/she will be.

What Gives Values Their Value

Now, our "values" are as transcendent as Moses's tables, but their transcendence is turned upside down. They don't come from above, from Sinai or from the heavens, but from underneath. They are not handed over to us by some active power; we are the agents. But are we really? Are values human? For they might even be subhuman.

I pointed out above that ancient thought saw in human excellence an example of a wider principle that holds good for any living being.[9] In a way that resembles ancient thought, modern thought since Thomas Hobbes has been seeing in decency hardly more than the result of a desire for self-preservation that is to be found in any living being. And later thinkers, in the wake of Darwin, interpret decency as the result of a process of natural selection that makes us prefer what enhances the life of the species. This comes to a head in the late modern doctrine of value, put forward with great clarity by Nietzsche: values are set by the will to power as the conditions of possibility of its unfolding.[10] Still more recently, sociobiology endeavors to explain to what extent morality was an advantage in the struggle for life of the human groupings against a hostile natural surrounding.

The present-day Western cast of mind is very much influenced by this view of what makes a value what it is. Hence the idea that some values are "our" values. Behind this possessive pronoun, which sounds merely descriptive and therefore quite harmless at first blush, lies in hiding a whole view of the origin of our moral evaluations. In particular,

"European values" could boil down to be what ensures the perpetuation of a European way of life. But what if this way of life, together with the values that make it possible, should prove to be scarcely more than folklore, quaint ways of quaint people, soooooo exciting for tourists, but keeping clear from any claim to a universal worth? Scottish gentlemen wear filibegs, others don't; French people eat frogs, others don't; Europeans as a whole (should) respect women and treat them as equal to the male, others don't, and so on. The common talk about the defense of our European values over against the supposedly worthless values of other people very quickly becomes a way to cling to one's privileges. Little wonder that other cultures turn the tables on us and praise their own values.

Virtues as Commanded

What do we need for the West to go on taking itself seriously, together with what it stands for? How can we responsibly propose this to the rest of the world without indulging in cultural imperialism?

My hunch is that we should, to begin with, say good-bye to the very idea of "values." It goes without saying that we should keep as a precious treasure the *content* of these so-called values, for getting rid of this moral content may lead to our own undoing. But we should free this positive core from the suspicion of being hardly more than the folklore of the white man. In order to do that, we need to come back to the two premodern notions mentioned above, that is, virtues and commandments. Instead of playing the ones against the others, we should attempt a synthesis that would let them foster each other.

Now, as a matter of fact, this synthesis is not something that we have to construct. It already existed in the Middle Ages in the three religions. Let us think of some examples: Saint Ambrosius, in the late fourth century, simply cribbed Cicero's *De officiis*.[11] In the thirteenth century, Aquinas integrated the moral doctrines of the ancient philosophers into the part of his *Summa theologica* that deals with the four cardinal virtues, and Roger Bacon quoted large batches of Seneca in his *Moralis philosophia*.[12] Let us mention, too, similar attempts in the Arabic-speaking world, like the whole tradition of the treatises on the refinement of the mores (*Tahḏīb al-aḫlāq*). The most famous is the work of the Persian historian and philosopher Miskawayh, but other people took up the same thread, including the Christian philosopher and theologian Ibn 'Adī.[13] In his *Mīzān al 'Amal* (Scales of action), al-Ghazali, who was hardly a friend of philosophers, has a reasoned catalog of virtues that draws heavily on Greek philosophical ethics.[14] And finally, let us not forget, in the Jewish communities, Maimonides's reinterpretation of Jewish ethics in his *Eight Chapters*.[15] It paved the way for the whole modern enterprise of a redefinition of Judaism as an "ethical monotheism" (Leo Baeck).

For us, this supposes a double effort, to rethink both what virtues and what commandments are all about. On the one hand, we should endeavor to understand that virtues are the flourishing of the human as such, regardless of the diversity of cultures and religions. This implies acknowledging something like a human nature. On the other hand, we should get rid of the representation of God's commandments as "heteronomy." To put it in simpler terms, avoiding any term of art, those commandments are not the whims of a tyrant, foisted upon a fold of slaves. All the biblical commandments stem from a first basic and utterly simple commandment, namely "Be!," "Be what you are!" The "Become who you are" did not have to wait for Pindar, let alone for Nietzsche.[16] Whatever sounds like a legal ruling in the Bible is the small change of creation or, if you prefer, its refraction in different media that unfold the abilities implied therein.[17] This interpretation almost reached the level of a conscious, reflective thought in the Bible itself, for instance when Deuteronomy summarizes all the commandments to be observed under the heading of "choose life" (30:19).

In the present day, Western mankind is badly in need of this double rediscovery and recovery: on the one hand, of the virtues as being good for each and every human being, and on the other hand, of obedience to the commandment to be, and to be what one is. May it understand this necessity and this urgency.

The Family

The first place in which people are taught virtues and commanded to obey a benevolent being is the family. I possess, on the subject of the family, a minimal competence, mainly practical in nature: I am a married man. But even in this field my expertise is limited: I can tell you that the first forty-eight years of married life are just great. Of what comes afterward, I have not the foggiest idea.

The Family under Fire

To put it bluntly: the family is feeling the flak. It is menaced at the same time from the inside and from the outside, in a constant feedback loop. The inner weaknesses of individuals—due to character and mores—and outside circumstances, mainly institutional, take advantage of and reinforce each other, in a vicious circle that very well could destroy the family.

As for the facts, since I hate it when people belabor the obvious, I will cut my story short: Western societies are witnessing the crumbling down of the so-called traditional form of the family, a form which is in fact relatively recent. The growing rates of divorce, premarital sex, extramarital relationships and births, single parenthood, not to mention the alleged "same-sex families," all belong to this large-scale phenomenon. This movement is not from yesterday. It hails back several decades, not to say several centuries.

As for the causes, two institutions, the modern state and the market, can't help trying to break the family and to recast it according to their own needs. Destroying the family is part of their more or less unspoken agenda. This has hardly anything to do with the will of their upholders, who may be, in their private life, exemplary participants in their families. The only reason is that the family doesn't fit into the inner logic that pushes the state and the market forward, toward the full implementation of their own logic. Now, those two institutions are the two most powerful of modern times.

The family already was menaced by Plato's communist utopia in the *Republic*. Common ownership of goods and of women was expected to lead to the perfect *polis*, the perfect city-state. Nevertheless, what Plato's Socrates aimed at was more the generalization of family relationships than their abolition. Every child should treat every woman as his mother and every man as his father.[1]

The modern state has another strategy. It tries to reduce human beings to individuals. Its early modern form, absolute monarchy, reduced them to individuals who pay and obey, that is, to subjects. In its late modern form, to individuals who pay and vote, that is, to citizens. An important example of this is the integration into the French one-and-indivisible nation of the Jews living on the French territory. According to the celebrated formula of Stanislas, Earl of Clermont-Tonnerre, in his speech of December, 23, 1789, this was supposed to grant every right to the Jews as individuals while refusing them every special right (privilege) as communities (Il faut refuser tout aux Juifs comme nation et accorder tout aux Juifs comme individus).[2] It is interesting that on the issue of how to articulate to each other the relationship between the individual and the state, the Jewish people, which is not just any people, should have assumed the role of a paradigm. In any case, the political institutions of the French Revolution tended to create a society of "equal and disjoint atoms."[3] As for the consequences, I need not refer to the famous chapter that Tocqueville devoted to "individualism."[4]

The democratic form that the modern state has taken for at least two centuries still enhances the emphasis on the individual. By depriving the nobility of its privileges, it loosened the bonds between generations. By making inheriting more difficult by means of heavier and heavier taxation, it makes wealth more liquid. A total abolition of inheritance would deal the family a mortal blow or, at least, reduce it to the dimension of the contemporary. One can argue on behalf of inheritance and against it, and in both cases with very good reasons: (a) it is absurd and revolting that some children should be born "with a silver spoon in the mouth," endowed with advantages which others are deprived of simply because the former only "had to take the trouble to be born";[5] (b) it is absurd and revolting to think that hardworking people should not be allowed to transmit the fruit of their labor to their offspring but that instead they should let the state redistribute it to the children of idle people. Everything depends on the point of view.

The state is not the only power that threatens the family. The market, too, tries to reduce people to individuals who sell and buy, to consumers for whom whatever exists has to be considered as a commodity that has a price. The sovereignty of market and of money can be looked at as the final stage of the war waged against aristocracy, first by the French kings, then by the French Revolution. The German poet H. Heine ironically gave to the three men who were the greatest levelers of human history the name of the three "R's": Richelieu, Robespierre, and . . . Rothschild. In the seventeenth century, the French cardinal and statesman brought the country squires to heel to the advantage of the central royal power; in the eighteenth century, his fellow countryman, attorney before the revolution and politician during it, sent a great many of the gentry's members to the guillotine; and finally, in the nineteenth century, the Austrian banker dealt the landed gentry the last blow by depriving it of its means of subsistence.[6]

Behind its visible influence, and for the most part unbeknownst to us, the market introduces its own patterns of thought into the holy precinct of the family. You replace your old crate with the latest model. Why shouldn't you junk your old hag and replace her with a younger girl?—to be sure, provided you can afford to do so. In our societies, divorce is becoming a sign of social promotion, faithfulness to one's husband or wife a sign of poverty or lack of stamina and/or imagination.

The answer to that is obvious: a car is only a *thing*; a woman is a *person*. This is very true, and even trite. But this is precisely the distinction that the market tends to erase by reducing whatever exists to the level of commodities.

What the Family Alone Can Do

In the teeth of all those attacks, the family has a stronghold. There is a realm in which the family can hardly be replaced, namely the reproduction of the human species. Even if one can imagine a totalitarian state in which children would not grow in their families, but exclusively under the care of professional educators, they are begotten by a male and a female of the species.

Some utopias, or some nightmares, dream of doing away with natural reproduction by letting human beings grow like sprouts in glass bottles. We all know Aldous Huxley's *Brave New World*, published in 1932. Less famous is the booklet in which a very competent scientist, the British biologist J. B. S. Haldane, in 1923, first described what he named "ecto-genesis," that is, reproduction in vitro, outside of the maternal womb.[7]

Because of the part it plays in reproduction, the family articulates two dimensions of our being that don't necessarily get on well together, the biological and the cultural. It is grounded on reproduction, which is a plain biological phenomenon. At the same time, the family raises the children and introduces them into the sphere of what transcends the biological level: first, language, then morals, and finally literature, art, and religion.

The biological bond is something that can't be erased. Precisely because it is not chosen, it subsists in spite of everything. Hence a very important moral consequence: a family is a space inside of which people are accepted for what they *are*, and not for what they *do*. To be sure, parents are far more satisfied when their children are healthy and successful and behave well. But the parents of a person with a disability, of a dropout, of a criminal don't love him or her less. Parents who are worthy of the name can distinguish; they can draw a firm line between what their children *do* and what their children *are*. They may, and they even should, try to cure the handicap, to remedy the professional failures, to make their child forsake his or her evil doings. But the person remains or should remain the object of an unconditional love.

Now, this is exactly what other authorities, be they the civil society or the state, can't afford to do. They can't give each of their members the same share in goods and honor. They may ensure a minimum for each to be able to live decently. But they have to give more to those who produce more. This "more" can consist of economic advantages—in short, money. It can be symbolic rewards, like honor, memberships, and so on. One can mix the two, like awards, medals, and prizes. Doing otherwise wouldn't be merely scarcely efficient; it would be unjust, too.

The dimension according to which there is something in us that possesses an intrinsic worth is the personal dimension. A person is a being that we can and should respect as such, regardless of their performances. Now, what produces persons is the family.

Hence, two cheers and a half for the family.

Where Is the Ultimate Goal?

Where does the last half-cheer linger?

The family is not an end in itself. First, because it is not a beginning. In other words, we don't *make* children. Today, it is common parlance in French to speak as if children were things that we produce: we say now "to make children" (faire *des enfants*). We used to say: "to have children" (avoir *des enfants*). In this phrase, "having" did not mean possessing them. We get them, we *receive* them, as the German has it (*bekommen*, or, in colloquial language, *kriegen*). We may call the authority from which we receive them God, Nature, the species, evolution, or the like. This doesn't make—on this point at least—any significant difference. We don't make our children what they are, and don't make them what we want them to be, either. They have to decide what they will be. To be sure, it is our duty to give them the best possible education. But the ultimate choice will be theirs. For believers, I should say, the ultimate goal of educating children is their ultimate beatitude, that is, in traditional language, the salvation of their souls. The Bible is not that sweet on the family. It is full of stories of incest, adulteries, and bastards. Its principles are severe: man will have to leave father and mother and cleave to his wife (Gen. 2:24). Jesus, too, has harsh words against people who prefer their family to the kingdom of heaven (Matt. 10:37; 12:48).

I pedantically said "beatitude." I did not say "happiness." The goal is not the happiness of the persons. For the snag about happiness is that it is never reached when you set it as your goal. When you say: "I will neglect everything, provided that I am happy," this simply doesn't work. The good life may bring about happiness, but does not produce it automatically. To put it in Kant's words: morals can make us worthy of being happy; but they can't warrant that we will enjoy the happiness that we deserve.[8]

Now, families produce goods that are intrinsically better and more lasting than the material goods that any factory can turn out or the services that any agency can put at our disposal. The person is longer lived than any enterprise. For religious people, who believe that the person is invited freely to enter into an eternal communion with God, what is most personal in the person—in religious vocabulary, the "soul"—is even longer lived than a civilization and even than the universe itself. In family enterprises, for instance, there may arise—not to say that there always arise—conflicts between the family dimension and the enterprise dimension that they endeavor to bring together. The children are not always willing to take up the trade of their parents, nor are they always able to get the necessary competence. The basic rule is that we don't beget managers—or, for that matter, chimney sweepers or pianists—but free persons. Those persons *may* wish to ply the same trade as their parents, but they *need* not. Compelling them to stay in the same ruts as their parents simply doesn't work. It produces only frustration. The ultimate goal is not the survival of the family enterprise. To be sure, such a survival is a very good thing, but it is not *the* Good, full stop. This conflict of interests in the example of family enterprises is hardly more than a particular aspect of a more general tension between the family and what we call at present "society."

Idea of "Society"

The history of the word "society" teaches us something important. Originally, in the late Middle Ages, the Latin word *societas* meant a commercial association, that is, a company. Free and adult human beings, male for the most part, necessarily men of property, joined their efforts in order to invest money, for example shipowners in overseas business.

We have been trained for centuries to call the human community "society," hence to think of it on the model of a company. The apex of this view of the human community as a society is the theory of the social contract, according to which society arises out of a compact or covenant between persons who decide freely either to divest themselves of their rights and to bestow them on the sovereign (Hobbes) or to constitute a collective being (Rousseau).[9] Now, this can't possibly take place at the most basic level. In his treatise on politics—which was, by the way, the first ever written on this topic, and in which he coined the name of this science—Aristotle wrote what sounds like a truism: "Politics does not produce men, but receives them from nature."[10] Hence, the model of the being-together of human beings as a "society" is dreadfully inadequate as soon as we ask how we become members of the human community. For we do that by being born into it, which is certainly not the result of our choice.

As a consequence, people who look at the human community from the point of view of "society" must have misgivings about the family. On the one hand, society has to take the family for granted. On the other hand, it has to undermine the family. We may be grasping here the deepest reason for the animosity of the modern state and of the market against the family that I pointed out earlier.[11] Now, the model of society has its limits and will soon reach them in the most concrete way. Society is excellent on one point: enabling people who are already there to get on well together. But, on the other hand, it has nothing to say on a very important point, that is, nothing less than the very existence of mankind. It can tell us how we have to behave in order to keep living. But it can't answer a simple, but capital question: Why is there to be human life on this earth? What about the future of mankind?

Time and the Family

The matter of time is the point on which the family could have its say and does have something very precious to teach us. It is a peculiar, and even unique, relationship to time that very well could be applied to other levels of human life, and even become its cornerstone.

In former societies, the leading model of the family was the aristocratic one. A family was first and foremost a lineage, a vertical succession from father to son. The hero of P. G. Wodehouse's Blandings novels, the fluffy-minded Lord Emsworth, understands himself as "Clarence Threepwood, ninth earl of Emsworth." His first duty was to beget a potential tenth earl. This outlook on life is symbolized by the gallery of ancestors whose portraits hang in the stateroom of the castle. Elsewhere in Western culture, the same outlook produces the powerful image of the family tree, in particular the tree of Jesse (Isa. 11:1), so beautifully represented on the stained-glass windows of many of our cathedrals.

Family ethics left little room for individual decisions. Marriages were arranged by the parents of the bride and of the groom, as they still are in many countries today. The West, with its idea that marriages should be grounded on mutual love between two responsible persons, is more an exception than a rule. Interestingly, the Catholic Church played an important part in allowing people to receive the sacrament of marriage without the consent of their parents, provided they decided freely to enter the bond of wedlock. What social pressure had been in charge of came thereby to be entrusted to the intelligence and moral sense of the persons. This was a mighty wager that evidenced a boundless trust in human freedom.

Aristocratic societies belong to the past. But their view of life should be kept as a precious treasure if we want to avoid the dire diagnosis of Edmund Burke that "people will not look forward to posterity, who never look backward to their ancestors," or that of Alexis de Tocqueville, who, one generation later, took up almost the same formula in his famous *Democracy in America*.[12]

Now, it is the case that our modern, democratic societies don't possess any institution that is in charge of caring about the very long run. What present-day politicians call the "long run" boils down to being the stretch between two elections. Democracy implies a frequent control by the voters and the possibility of "throwing out the rascals." This is an excellent thing. But it reduces the possibilities of real action to a tiny spell of time. This implies that decisions that may steer a country for a very long time will be taken by people who wield an ephemeral power. This is a great pity, because important problems develop at a very slow tempo. Which makes them seldom visible to the naked eye. Problems of demography, of the management of natural resources and of ecology, of education and culture at large, of religion have as their smallest unit of measure, say, ten years.

Traditional societies were for the most part ruled by a monarch. The king or queen understood him- or herself as part of a dynasty, as the heir of a series of ancestors. They tried to make this series as long as possible, with the result that upstarts had to forge dignified forebears, which they were not loath to do. On the other hand, to be precise in the other direction, toward the future, kings and queens had to preserve the reign—considered as a family property of sorts—for their offspring. They tried to enlarge it, or at least to bequeath it to their son without a loss. They thought in the long run, not because of special moral qualities, but simply because they couldn't possibly do otherwise, and they had to think that way because the underlying model for their whole practice was the family.

Who Cares?

The great British economist Lord John Maynard Keynes famously quipped in 1924 that "this long run is a misleading guide to current affairs. In the long run we are all dead."[13] Every person in charge, be he or she civil servant, moderator of a talk show, or whatnot, uses the "long run" in order to nip in the bud every attempt at speculating on the long-term consequences of policies. Obviously, Keynes spoke with his tongue in his cheek. Yet we should take the content of his statement seriously and ask: Is this a marvelously pliable truism, or a cowardly cop-out?

In the process of deciding, everything hinges upon how we understand the pronoun "we" in "*we* are all dead." If we mean the persons who are living today, this is undoubtedly true. Most probably, this was the idea that Keynes wanted to convey. This is suggested by the use he makes of the present tense: "we *are* dead" instead of "we *shall be* dead." If we think of the totality of the human species, "we human beings," this may still be true, but the "we" has a larger playground, in which a millennium is a puny thing. The real question is whether we can go beyond the boundary of our "I," for instance in the direction of our immediate offspring and of later generations. As the context makes clear, Keynes pleaded for an immediate intervention of state powers and poked fun at economists who claimed that things would settle down anyway. Are we allowed to quote him in support of an argument for dodging an urgent reflection? A reflection that would deal with what *we* could do *now* in order that *others* should be able, *in the future*, to live well and perhaps to live at all?

In the present-day world, the institutions that think in the very long run are not that many. Religious leaders do. Rabbis understand themselves as keeping alive a law that was given some three thousand years ago. Christian churches understand themselves as bearing witness to an event, the resurrection of the crucified Christ, which took place some two thousand years ago. Imams do the same for a *shariʿa* that originates in events that took place fourteen centuries ago. The ultimate goal of all those institutions is a salvation that transcends time.

In the secular realm, some civil servants can afford to set their sights on a remote future, because they do not depend directly on political changes of weather, but may stay behind the same desk for some thirty years. Among them, there are people who care for the future of their country, of the West, or of mankind at large. Some companies may outlive their founder, because the continuity of the brand they chose as their name is at stake. Their managers will endeavor to keep the reputation of the company as high as possible and for the longest possible stretch of time.

The family could provide other fields of human action with a useful model. Let us think for example of the ecological movement. It has taught us to look at the earth as the common heritage of mankind, as something that we received from the generations above, and even from the whole evolutionary process of life, and that we should feel committed to transmit unspoiled to the next generations. Edmund Burke wrote in 1790:

> One of the first and most leading principles on which the commonwealth and the laws are consecrated is, lest the temporary possessors and life-renters in it, unmindful of what they have received from their ancestors or of what is due to their posterity, should act as if they were the entire masters, that they should not think it among their rights to cut off the entail or commit waste on the inheritance

by destroying at their pleasure the whole original fabric of their society, hazarding to leave to those who come after them a ruin instead of an habitation—and teaching their successors as little to respect their contrivances as they had themselves respected the institutions of their forefathers.[14]

The great Irish statesman wrote these lines as a critique of the French Revolution, just one year after its outbreak. He thought of political systems. What he said may be obsolete now in the political realm. But it could be applied very easily to other fields, for example our planet as the common heritage of mankind.

CHAPTER NINE

Civilization as Conservation and Conversation

Culture gets a concrete realization in time and space as a definite civilization. But the latter word possesses at the same time a laudatory meaning, in which case it designates the peaceful and refined state of affairs among people, a state that we distinguish from the raw and warlike nature of what we call "barbarism." We feel it is our duty to stave it off in order thereby to defend "civilization." We are not the first who felt and acted that way. Many were the authors in the thirties who warned against Leninism, Fascism, and Nazism as being a new kind of barbarism. Nowadays, new threats, such as terrorism, are perceived as harbingers of one more comeback of barbarism. Hence, it is apposite that we should think about this trite opposition of barbarism/civilization.

A Word

For us, the adjective "barbarian" is fraught with all kinds of unpleasant connotations that conflate it with cruelty, disorder, and so on and generally refer to a sinking of the cultural level. This is the way in which Johan

Huizinga defined "barbarization" in his work of 1935 when he described it as "a cultural process through which an intellectual [*geestelijk*] state of high value that had been reached is gradually invaded and pushed back by elements of lower worth."[1] The great Dutch historian obviously had in mind the Nazi menace that already loomed large. It was to materialize and take over the whole of Europe some years later—and held him in detention. But the use of the word has a broader extent.

Probably, this is a consequence of the historical fact of the "barbarian invasions" that put a stop to the Roman Empire, or rather of the way in which the events that received this name were kept as a trauma by European memory. Since Rome and, later on, Europe in its wake understood themselves as the civilized part of the world, "barbarian" took a negative shade. We are still under the sway of this trauma, and we are constantly tempted to think of our present predicament along the same lines. We feel ourselves as civilized people menaced by barbarians all around, in the same way as the Chinese saw themselves as occupying the Middle Kingdom as a perfect circle and surrounded with inferior people of all ilks, who occupy the four corners of the square in which the Chinese circle is inscribed.

We can elicit a working concept of barbarism from the etymology of the word, provided we take it seriously. As is well known, it is first and foremost a linguistic notion which designates persons or human groups whose language is unintelligible for us, so that we imagine that they simply emit some onomatopoeia and go "br, br, br" with their tongues. This is a common practice in any linguistic area.[2] For instance, the Russian word for "German," немец (nemets), stems from the Indo-European root *NEM-, which means "to be dumb," like the Russian немой (nemoy). What is especially interesting in Slavic peoples and what singles them out from other ones is that they also reflectively found a name for themselves on the basis of the same image: they understand themselves, from the inside, as the people whose language is intelligible, hence as "the speaking people," from the root *SLAV-.

Originally, the adjective "barbarian" was a merely descriptive way to characterize people, without any value judgment as its underpinning. As a consequence, its use can function in two ways. The Latin poet Ovid, exiled among the fishers of the Black Sea, writes that he is there the barbarian, because the local people don't understand his speech.[3]

But it quickly became value laden, if we consider the Greek use of the word. Insofar as the Greeks considered themselves as superior, non-Greek-speaking human beings were banned to a lower rung on the scale of mankind. It would be difficult nowadays to strip the adjective "barbarian" of its negative connotation.

Now, I suggest that we should do better justice to the etymology by taking it seriously and drawing from it some deeper meaning.

Conversation

Barbarism means more and worse than a lack of ability to communicate, which is a bare fact. The latter, merely negative in nature, we could call "savagery," the raw state of human beings supposed to have been living in forests—as indicated by the word's origin in the Latin *silva*, "wood," "grove." Barbar*ism*, as the suffix suggests, is a deliberate stance. It is a refusal to communicate. Or, in its milder form, it consists in pretending that the gap is unbridgeable. As a consequence, its contrary, civilization, must have something to do with linguistic communication. Where conversation is not made possible by linguistic communication, violence is almost inevitable. "Cutting dead" is the first step toward the real killing. This will be my main thesis: civilization means basically *conversatio civilis*. *Conversatio civilis* is a notion that has a long and winding history,[4] and conversation at large is a theme that has attracted attention for some years, for instance that of literary scholars like the French Marc Fumaroli and philosophers like the British Roger Scruton.[5] The former dealt with it from the point of view of the history of ideas and mores and unraveled the progress of this ideal of peaceful and friendly communication between scholars beyond the boundaries of the different states that generated the common world of the Renaissance and later the *République des lettres* of the seventeenth century.[6]

The phrase began its career, probably, with Thomas Aquinas's critique of Averroës's thesis of an immediate communion of all minds in the Agent Intellect, which, says Aquinas, would jeopardize every *conversatio civilis*.[7] This rebuttal of Averroës's position implies that understanding is not spontaneous, not taken for granted, but is a task to be fulfilled by undertaking some sort of work. This is the basic condition of hermeneutics. Hermeneutics is not about how we understand each other. It deals with what is to be done once we understand that we *don't* understand.

Civilization designates an ideal of communication. Not just any kind of communication, but one which is thought of on the model of what obtains or should obtain in the city, among people who all enjoy the quality of *civis*, and hence deserve to be called *civilis*. A city is precisely that: a space defined by the possibility of linguistic communication, a space whose goal is to make communication between people possible, and even easy and spontaneous. Its ideal is the flourishing of human communication.

It might be interesting to point out that the same link between the two notions of a city and of civilized life was seen and expressed clearly in a totally different linguistic area than our Greco-Roman world. The Arabic philosophers, among several words that roughly correspond to our idea of what "civilization" is, coined a word that fits ours exactly, that is, *tamaddun*, based on the Arabic word for "city," *madīna*. The word doesn't simply mean "urbanization," as the material fact that nomads give up their vagrant life, settle down, and build permanent houses that constitute towns. The philosophers, in the ranks of whom I include Ibn Khaldun, are careful to observe that this process is a consequence of political life, man being a political animal according to that term's definition by Aristotle, which they begin by quoting approvingly. A city can even be said, tautologically, to civilize itself (*tatamaddanu al-madīna*).[8] Civilization arises from the political nature of human beings, which stems from their ability to handle *logos*. It represents the most perfect stage in the unfolding of their abilities to converse.

Hence the noble dream of a city that would encompass the whole of mankind, and even the gods, binding them through an all-pervading *logos*: the *cosmopolis* first conceived by the Stoics.[9] At its peak, conversation transcends the boundaries of the state, and even of mankind. Let us keep this idea in the back of our minds, for I will have to get back to it later on.

What motivates people who understand their caring for civilization as the cornerstone of their overall conservative attitude is the care for this civil conversation. Everything will hinge upon a pun. If I may ask for permission to give new life to a rather rare word by simply swapping two consonants, like some sort of deliberate spoonerism, I should venture the following formula: what is conservative is basically "conversative." The word is in the *Oxford English Dictionary*, by the way.[10] On the other hand, the *OED* fortunately ignores the "conversatism" that I might have been tempted to use. Conservation makes sense if and perhaps only if it enables conversation. Conservatism as a defense of conservation is justified if it contributes to fostering and enlarging conversation. Some sort of dialectics is at work here, a dialectics that can be observed at the humble level of everyday life. If we are willing to go on living with other people or if we are stuck with others in the same waiting room or blocked in an elevator, we will soon have to speak with them, unless we want to get either bored stiff or grumpy. If, conversely, we engage in a conversation with a perfect stranger, we more often than not will observe that our dialogue partner has interesting things to tell us. And therefore we will wish to conserve him or her or, possibly, it.

Are Civilization and Barbarism Real Antagonists?

Pitting civilization and barbarism against each other might be too blunt a way to handle the problem. Can too much civilization bring about barbarism? Is there a dialectic of civilization, analogous to Adorno and Horkheimer's well-known "Dialectic of the Enlightenment"? Giambattista Vico already spoke of the "barbarism of reflection."[11]

Let me take the example of another Italian, the great classical scholar and lyric poet Giacomo Leopardi. He contends that barbarism is a condition of civilization, first because it precedes civilization in time, second because the luxury of some is made possible by the toil of others.[12] Extreme civilization brings about extreme barbarism. Barbarian peoples vanquish the civilized ones because the latter are full of grand illusions.[13] At a deeper level still, he develops a whole dialectics between *civiltà* and *barbarie*. According to Leopardi, reason destroys the illusions without which man can't live, leading thereby to its own contrary, barbarism.[14] Reason has a propensity to occupy the whole soul. It takes its bearings from any principle and pushes it till its last consequences, even when it contradicts nature. Reason is often a source of barbarism, and in its excess, it is always so.[15] Human history is a continuous shift from one level of civilization to another one, then to excess of civilization, finally to barbarism, and then back again to the lowest level of civilization.[16] The best state is a middle civilization (*civiltà media*), a balance between reason and nature.[17] Leopardi expresses this in a gorgeous formula: reason must shed light, but not commit arson.[18]

As a consequence, there is a temptation to call on the barbarians, or rather people who are supposed to be barbaric in their mores, to rejuvenate cultures that grow old. This is an old temptation. I stumbled on it in Herder, who turns the common representation of the Roman Empire being flooded by barbarian invasions topsy-turvy into the positive image of new blood flowing into the aging body.[19] Since the invaders were Germans, one may suspect a certain amount of *pro domo* pleading.

A related idea is still to be found under the pen of a fellow countryman of Herder, namely Martin Heidegger, in the famous Black copybooks. For him, barbarism is not the worst danger, the latter being the attempt at salvaging the "higher values of culture" on the raft of Christianity.[20] He considers that "culture" is the fundamental form of barbarism.[21] Barbarism does not consist in the people being primitive and deprived of culture, but in the people being educated or, to quote a Nazi civil servant, in their being "educated" while remaining vulgar.[22] In an early note of around 1934, he even considers national socialism, or rather the image thereof which he was still dreaming of, as "a barbarian principle," barbarism being what is essential in, and is the greatness of, national socialism.[23]

Let me make two observations. Both are historical, but they bear on our present situation. The first deals with the positive effect of barbarian invasions. We must distinguish. The so-called barbarian invasions may have had a positive effect on the culture of late antiquity. This was the case because the Germans and other invaders wanted to enter the Roman Empire not to destroy it but to share in its benefits. More concretely, their leaders wanted to become part of the Roman nobility.[24] This implied these leaders' partially renouncing their "identity," that is, their sacrificing some of their customs. My ancestors, real or alleged, the Gallic tribes, forsook their charming custom of burning alive the human victims of their offerings to their gods.[25] This is very much to their credit, that they felt the superiority of another culture and didn't stick to their own. On the other hand, some barbarians, really barbaric in nature, want to destroy the culture into which they are admitted and to replace it with a culture of their own. When the Mongol riders, who were nomads, wanted to convert the cultivated fields of Europe into pastures for their horses, they could scarcely be considered as contributing to the progress of civilization.

The second observation deals with the very origin of the European cast of mind. Two currents ran parallel among the Greeks: one defends the superiority of the Greeks; one admits the worth of a *barbaros philosophia*, supposed to be extant among Indians or Jews.[26] Whether the Greeks took this really seriously or with their tongue in their cheek is an issue that should not detain us here. In any case, however, the very fact that they played with the hypothesis of their possible inferiority may be the best proof of the real superiority of Greek culture. Barbarians are people who consider themselves civilized. Civilized people are those who understand that, under the thin veneer of their own culture, barbarism keeps menacing them from the inside and has to be constantly kept at bay by a protracted effort.

Continuity

Refusal to communicate—that is, barbarism—is part and parcel of a larger stance toward Being at large, which is refusal of *continuity*. This comes to the fore especially in our stance toward the past. A deliberate break with the past brings about a loss of civilization and is the harbinger of some form of barbarism, the latter word being understood in the usual meaning as well, that is, as stupidity and cruelty. The historical examples of such a fact are many. Among them, the French Revolution may have pride (or shame) of place.

This was seen very clearly by Edmund Burke. He stressed the importance of continuity in human affairs, although the word occurs only once in his masterpiece. He considers barbarism as the result of a lack of continuity. He views society as a contract, in the wake of the tradition of early modern political philosophy from Hobbes and Rousseau, not to mention the later Sir Henry Maine. But he enlarges the scope of such a contract. The theorists of modern political philosophy more or less imagine that the social contract is the result of the agreement of people who were born by a spontaneous generation of sorts, in Lucretius's style,[27] and are together at the same time, in the same way as players around a whist table. Burke conceives of the contract as obtaining between "those who are living, those who are dead, and those who are to be born."[28]

Among the most fundamental rights of mankind, there is one that might be the first, although it was discovered and formulated as such rather late and remained in the margins. This is the right to continuity. It was powerfully orchestrated by the Spanish philosopher José Ortega y Gasset, in his *La rebelión de las masas* (The rebellion of the masses), which won him international acclaim.[29] But the philosopher had borrowed his central formula—which he acknowledged with perfect honesty—from a Frenchman who is now fallen into an almost total oblivion, by the name of Charles Dupont-White (1807–78). In the preface that he added to his translation of John Stuart Mill's *On Liberty*, Dupont-White wrote the following words: "La continuité est due à l'homme." In the second edition, he exchanged this formula for the bolder and, in my opinion, far more felicitous one that Ortega quoted: "La continuité est un droit de l'homme"; continuity is a human right.[30]

It might be apposite here to tell a personal remembrance about how I got a more positive view of what conservatism is all about. Not that many years ago, I had to undergo an operation, and they took away from my body a matter of one foot of bowels. You may have guessed already that I survived the operation. . . . Now, the surgeon told me afterward that he certainly could have removed still a greater part of them. But, he told me, "I uphold a conservative kind of surgery." This meant—and the phrase is common parlance among physicians—that he tried to keep as much of an organ as could be kept without endangering the life and health of the patient. On the other hand, he didn't hesitate to cut away whatever could have had negative or even lethal consequences for the people whom he had to deal with.

What I am driving at with this short story is that continuity is not fixity, is not the stubborn clinging to what already is. On the contrary, it is the will to go on. Let me venture a small but significant step: it is the will to *carry on* in the literal meaning of the verb, that is, to transfer goods from one point to another. This implies bringing what is to bear on what isn't yet and should come into being, bringing the legacy of the past to bear on the future. In a word: making history. History is a form of conversation.

History

All this presupposes that the past, or whatever came before us, is something with which we can and should engage in a conversation. Hence, it must have something to tell us, some meaning. The past can hardly be considered as a dustbin full to the brim of senseless errors that could and should be done away with and buried in oblivion. For the past has at least one great quality: it has produced us. Hence, it is an elementary duty that we should feel grateful toward it. We have to see in it a repository of many things, unequal in value, some even regrettable, but in no case systematically to be discarded on the trumped-up excuse that they belong to the past and are, as the American idiom has it, passé.

There is such a thing as historical barbarism, which is a will to forget, to weigh the anchors, to cast one's moorings in the past. Unfortunately, attempts at such an artificial forgetfulness crop up in our present days. In my country, reforms in the educational system give evidence of a deliberate intention to get rid of whatever constituted the reference points of our identity. France is not the only country that is menaced. There is a special case to be made for classical literature, which includes "classics" in the academic meaning of this word as well as the biblical heritage, the knowledge of and familiarity with which defined in former times, and for quite a long spell, the education that was expected to scour barbarism from us and lead us to civilization, according to Cicero's and Erasmus's ideal of the *literae humaniores*. Classical works, be they ancient ("pagan") or biblical, have a great advantage over against any other kind of literary learning. They contain in themselves the dialogue that constitutes civilization, for they are at the same time "we" and "other people," the ancestors we chose to adopt because we found that they had interesting things to tell us.

Historical studies have a tendency to change the past that still pulses in our veins into a corpse. They objectify the past and sort of kill it, since they emphasize what is different from us and by so doing deprive the past of whatever might feed and enrich us. Nietzsche saw this clearly in the second of his "untimely meditations."[31]

The adequate stance toward the past is some sort of conversation. On the one hand, tradition is living transmission. We can carry on because the past carries us forth. The past has made us. But, on the other hand, we to some extent make the past, we choose it as our own personal story, as leading to what we are now. This is the truth hidden in Jean-Paul Sartre's existentialism.[32] But historical science is there to help us correct this subjective appropriation and understand better and better that the past is infinitely richer and more colorful than the knowledge we can get of it at a definite point in time.

Let me here quote some sentences by the Russian poet Ossip Mandelstam, who died in 1937 on his way to the Gulag. They were written in the early twenties: "The affirmation and justification of existing values of the past is as much a revolutionary act as the construction of new values. . . . All the trouble happens when instead of the existing past with its deep roots arises 'the yesterday.'" Now, the "yesterday," according to the same poet, "does not exist"; it has to be. In Latin grammatical parlance, its tense is the *gerund* in which the poet wished to see his own mode of being.[33]

What has led to us is older than history, if we mean thereby the written records of the past, according to the received definition of history in contradistinction to prehistory. It is even older than the whole human adventure. It plunges its roots into the very long stretch of time that began with the so-called Big Bang. Our modern view of Nature has erased the boundary that separated history and nature, the transitory sublunary and the eternal. Nature herself is caught in an evolutionary process. This leads me to a further enlarging of the contrast that obtains between civilization and barbarism. A new partner enters the dialogue that constitutes civilization, a mighty partner, Nature herself.

Nature as Barbaric

Nature itself, the physical world in its breadth, has to be looked at as meaningful. Now, it is the case that we have been accustomed for a matter of two or three centuries to see in it hardly more than a battlefield or a chaos. Modern science, or a definite understanding of its achievements, has led us to see it as ruled by the law of the jungle only. Hilary Putnam reports a conversation at dinner in which somebody takes for granted that "the universe is an uncaring machine," wholly indifferent to our doings.[34] How this worldview became received wisdom, this is a story that I have told in a book that is now more than fifteen years old.[35] Darwinism, or a certain vulgar interpretation of it, invites us to interpret living beings as the mere product of chance, which is a nickname not of providence but of dumb natural mechanisms. Nature is barbarian.

As for us human beings, we are, together with the higher faculties that distinguish us from the other living beings, the mere products of natural selection. We are simply winners. We never deserved to get the jackpot. We simply had luck. "Luck" is the human name of "chance," and perhaps a mere anthropomorphism. This stance, which is basically intellectual in nature, may have practical consequences of the direst kind. Nature, such as we conceive of her, does not deserve our respect. And we don't give it to her, either. The modern outlook somehow takes up the Gnostic vision of a radical strangeness of man in the cosmos. We view ourselves as castaways, or as invaders, not as born gentlefolk, but as upstarts. And we behave as such, on the model, real or alleged, of barbarians who enter a higher culture. Since the dawn of the modern age, we have been barging into Nature's larder and plundering it.

A French philosopher whom I was so fortunate as to know personally, the late Michel Henry (d. 2002), bluntly called the modern project by the name of "barbarism." He put forward this idea in a book that he published in 1987 and that he entitled *La Barbarie*. Henry ascribed what he considered to be barbarian in modern times to the unmitigated triumph of the scientific worldview, Galileo's outlook. Galileo's intellectual revolution was triggered by a sea change that he expressed by a shift in the metaphor of the book of nature. He assumed that this book is written in mathematical language. At his time and age, this meant the language of Euclidean geometry, circles and squares.[36] Since then, mathematics and, in its wake, mathematical physics have made giant strides that deserve our admiration. But still, mathematics is not the language of our everyday experience of life. It leaves us in the lurch as to how to lead a meaningful life. Henry powerfully orchestrated the idea according to which this tearing asunder of the fabric of human experience leads to some kind of barbarism.[37]

Nature as Civilized

Now, poisonous substances can be turned into remedies if they are handled properly, according to the two-sidedness of the Greek tradition.

The evolutionary view of nature may help us to heal the wound that it has opened. This is a property that it shares with history. More deeply, it shares with the historical past, and even to a greater degree, the quite positive property of having brought us into being. It is in its whole hallowed backward by this result. For if it is not, whence could we draw our legitimacy?

Nature is something with which we sort of have to engage in a conversation, too. Let me here introduce some ideas that I found under the pen of Augustine. They are very discreetly expressed, rather en passant, and for this reason they were seldom taken up and elaborated upon by later thinkers. In my opinion, however, they deserve a thoughtful reading. The church father is dealing with the book of Genesis, or, more precisely, commenting upon Adam's task of working in and watching over paradise garden. This brings him to a meditation on agriculture, that is, of a human doing that which already was conceived of as a metaphor for culture at large. As early as Cicero, what we now call culture, *cultura animi*, was understood on the basis of a real etymology, as a way for us to till the soil of our own mind.[38] Says Augustine, "Is there a greater spectacle and more worthy of our wonder, or where human reason can more somehow speak with nature [*cum rerum natura humana ratio quodammodo loqui*], than when [through the activity of the peasant] the force of the root and of the seed is asked [*interrogatur*] about what it can do and what it can't . . . ?"[39] Agriculture is said to consist in some sort of dialogue with nature. Perhaps this could be said of culture at large. Nature answers the questions we ask her. Reason in us has its echo in the reason that is buried in the world. Nature is not dumb, or speaking a language that we don't understand—hence, barbarian—but, to quote another, earlier Latin church father, Lactantius, "Reason knows reason" (*rationem ratio cognoscit*).[40]

How is this possible? The Latin church fathers were heirs to the Latin Stoic tradition and had received from it the idea of "seminal reasons" (*logos spermatikos*). For people who believe in the Bible, "nature" is the nickname of creation. It is fraught with meaning, a meaning that we have to decipher. It is a language of sorts. This is expressed in the old metaphor of the book of nature, in its various uses along a rich and colorful history.[41]

Earlier in this book, I mentioned the idea of some medieval poets that the birds have a language of their own, that is, Latin.[42] The birds speak not just any vernacular, but the dignified language of higher administration and culture. This implies that they are not barbarians. To some extent, *we* are the barbarians, because we don't understand them. We can take the birds as a metonymy for Nature at large.

Nature as a Dialogue Partner

I don't recall to our memory those medieval ideas out of the antiquarian curiosity of an esthete. We badly need a balanced view of nature, one that could steer a middle course between two excesses, one that sees her as a corpse that we can cut up as we want and another that sees in her a goddess, like the Nature of the eighteenth-century *Philosophes* or the Gaia worshiped by some deep ecologists of the present time. One could venture the idea that the best stance toward Nature was the medieval one. According to a Jewish thinker like Maimonides as well as for Latin Scholasticism, Nature has her laws because things have a stable nature.[43] God does not have to bestow on them at each moment of time a bundle of properties, as in medieval Islam, in the so-called Kalām. By the way, the position of so-called creationism, which is rampant in the American Bible Belt and in large areas of the Islamic world, is very much the same as that of the medieval practitioners of Kalām.

But in the medieval worldview, things are created all the same; they depend on the will of God, who bestows on them Being. By this token, nature has the minimal consistency that enables it to become the adequate object of a science. But we thereby stave off the danger of foisting on Nature the too heavy load of independent existence, of Being out of oneself, what medieval thinkers called the property of *aseitas*.

We sort of have to consider as a task this intellectual comeback of the Middle Ages. The idea of creation might be the strongest bulwark against some sort of ontological barbarism. We are facing a choice between two kinds of *aseitas*. Two candidates vie for the title of *ens a se*, a being out of itself: the inanimate world of matter and God. If the former merits the title, we are the only speaking beings in a dumb world. The world can't understand us. And can we understand it? We certainly can discover the laws of its working, and we can write them in rigorous, mathematical language. But "understanding," properly speaking, means knowing the reason for which somebody acts. Modern science owes its spectacular achievements to the stance advertised by Bacon: putting into brackets any teleological outlook. Hence, we can manipulate things that we don't understand. To quote Claude Bernard's baffling formula: "Man can do more than he knows" (l'homme peut plus qu'il ne sait).[44] Because of this, we are barbarians in a barbaric world. Little wonder that we should behave like barbarians. On the other hand, if we choose the latter candidate for *aseitas*, that is, God, we can become the dialogue partners of a rational Being whose will underlies the whole show and who created in the *logos* that was "at the beginning"; we can engage in a conversation. This conversation with nature justifies our effort toward a conservation of nature as being the necessary condition of our being, and at the same time as somehow deserving to be preserved for her own sake.

Conclusion: Conserving Being

A conservative person is commonly supposed to be an enemy of freedom, or at least not to trust human freedom, to have pessimistic misgivings about it, so that he or she wants to put a stop on its progress.

In fact, conservative people are simply conscious of the weight that lies on the shoulders of man as a free being. They know that whatever bears the stamp of humanity, such as historical achievements, depends on the will of people to uphold them. If this will should fail, those achievements would crumble down and disappear forever. If I may indulge in punning—but puns can conceal deep truths—conservatism is a question of maintenance. In my native French, the verbs *conserver* and *maintenir* are not strictly synonyms, but they overlap to a large degree. Conservative is the person who is conscious of the necessity of a maintenance for human things in their wholeness.

Acknowledging the presence of *logos* in things might enable us to gain a broader concept of what conservatism is all about, while answering a common suspicion that the very idea of a conservative stance used to arouse. The critique was easy: "You claim to defend law and order, or anything whatsoever that you advertise as being valuable; in fact, you simply get cold feet when confronted with reforms or social upheavals of any kind that could endanger your position as a privileged member of a ruling elite, etc., etc." The same critique could be leveled against attempts at salvaging, say, Western civilization. For it could exactly as easily as in the former case be put forward that we can hardly assume that this culture deserves to be preserved. Its history is not made of marble, but of "living stones" that can be sinners. "Your alleged defense of civilization boils down to being a parochial enterprise, to the benefit of a small number." Now, what has to be salvaged is not a particular political system any longer, not even a definite civilization. It is mankind as a whole, the speaking animal, the conversing animal, that doubts of its own legitimacy and that needs grounds for wishing to push further the human adventure.

NOTES

Introduction

1. G. K. Chesterton, *Orthodoxy* [1908] (San Francisco: Ignatius Press, n.d.), ch. 3, p. 35.

2. Ibid., ch. 2, p. 24.

3. G. K. Chesterton, "Is Humanism a Religion?," in *The Thing* (London: Sheed and Ward, 1929), 16–17. The emphasis on "truth" is mine.

4. A. J. Balfour, *The Foundations of Belief* (London: Longmans, Green & Co., 1895), ch. 4, p. 83; C. Péguy, "De la situation faite au parti intellectuel dans le monde moderne devant les accidents de la gloire temporelle" [1907], in *Oeuvres en prose*, ed. R. Burac (Paris: Gallimard, 1988), 2:725. Balfour's idea is quoted in M. de Unamuno, *Del sentimiento trágico de la vida en los hombres y en los pueblos* [1913], ch. 2.

5. See A. Funkenstein, *Theology and the Scientific Imagination from the Late Middle Ages to the XVIIth Century* (Princeton: Princeton University Press, 1986), ch. 4.

6. See ch. 1, under "Project and Task."

7. See R. Brague, *The Anchors in the Heavens*, trans. B. Lapsa (South Bend, IN: St. Augustine's Press, forthcoming).

8. See R. Brague, *The Legitimacy of the Human*, trans. P. Seaton (South Bend, IN: St. Augustine's Press, 2017), 131–33 (end of ch. 7).

9. See R. Brague, *The Legend of the Middle Ages*, trans. L. Cochrane (Chicago: University of Chicago Press, 2009), 28–30.

10. This is the title of C. S. Lewis's extremely insightful introduction to his *English Literature in the Sixteenth Century Excluding Drama* (Oxford: Oxford University Press, 1954), 1–65.

11. Aesop, "The Two Bags" fable. See, for example, Cicero, *Tusculanae disputationes*, ed. G. Fohlen and J. Humbert (Paris: Les Belles Lettres, 1931), 3.30.73 (2:43), and, of course, Matt. 7:3–5.

12. See the beginning of the previous section, "Back to the Middle Ages?"

13. See R. Brague, *Le Règne de l'homme: Genèse et échec du projet moderne* (Paris: Gallimard, 2015), 12–15, trans. P. Seaton in *The Kingdom of Man: Genesis and Failure of the Modern Project* (Notre Dame, IN: University of Notre Dame Press, 2018).

Chapter One   The Failure of the Modern Project

1. J. Habermas, "Die Moderne—Ein unvollendetes Projekt" [1980], in *Kleine politische Schriften, I–IV* (Frankfurt: Suhrkamp, 1981), 444–64, especially 452–53.

2. See L. Dupré, *Passage to Modernity: An Essay in the Hermeneutics of Nature and Culture* (New Haven: Yale University Press, 1993), 101, 119, 126, 160; Dupré, *The Enlightenment and the Intellectual Foundations of Modern Culture* (New Haven: Yale University Press, 2004), 4; P. Manent, *Les Métamorphoses de la cité* (Paris: Flammarion, 2010), 9–11.

3. See H. Friedrich, *Montaigne* [German] (Bern: Francke, 1949), 419–25.

4. See A. Koyré, *Études d'histoire de la pensée scientifique* (Paris: Gallimard, 1966), 213–23 (on Galileo), 376–86 (on Pascal). Koyré's position is an extreme one, which was later qualified.

5. Galileo, *Dialogo sopra i due massimi sistemi del mondo*, ed. F. Flora (Milan: Mondadori, 1996), Second Day (p. 153).

6. F. W. Nietzsche, frag. 15 [51], in *Kritische Studienausgabe* [hereafter *KSA*] (Berlin: De Gruyter; Munich: dtv, 1980), 13:442; see also Ossip Mandelstam, "The Nineteenth Century," in Слово и культура [Slovo i kul'tura], in Стихотворения: Проза [Stikhotvorenija: Proza] (Moscow: EKSMO, 2011), 544; F. W. Nietzsche, frag. 25 [290], Spring 1884, in *KSA*, 11:85.

7. Descartes, letter to Mersenne, March 1636, in *Oeuvres Complètes*, ed. A. Adam and P. Tannery (Paris: Cerf, 1897), 1:339; Auguste Comte mentions the "great philosophical renovation, projected by Descartes and Bacon," in *Cours de philosophie positive*, ed. J. P. Enthoven (Paris: Hermann, 1975), 58th lesson (p. 639).

8. D. Defoe, *An Essay upon Projects* [1697], in *The True-Born Englishman, and Other Writings*, ed. P. N. Furbank and W. R. Owens (London: Penguin, 1997), 186 (capitals in the text), then 188.

9. Swift, *Gulliver's Travels*, World's Classics (Oxford: Oxford University Press, 1948), pt. 3, chs. 4–6, pp. 213–33.

10. Joseph Glanvill, *Plus ultra, or The Progress and Advancement of Knowledge since the Days of Aristotle* [. . .] (London: James Collins, 1668; reprint, Hildesheim: Olms, 1979), 8; M. Shelley, *Frankenstein* (London: Penguin, 1994), ch. 24, p. 204.

11. J.-P. Sartre, *L'Existentialisme est un humanisme* (Paris: Nagel, 1946), 55; see also 23, 69–70.

12. J.-P. Sartre, *Cahiers pour une morale* (Paris: Gallimard, 1983), 267.

13. See below, in the section "Being an Experiment," 16–18.

14. See, for instance, Tacitus, *Historiae*, ed. C. Halm (Leipzig: Teubner, 1989), 5.5 (p. 205).

15. See A. Maier, *Zwei Grundprobleme der scholastischen Naturphilosophie: Das Problem der intensiven Größe; Die Impetustheorie* (Rome: Storia e letteratura, 1951), 114–20.

16. R. Hannig, *Grosses Handwörterbuch Ägyptisch-Deutsch* (Mainz: von Zabern, 1997), 748b.

17. *The Story of Si-Nuhe* [Berlin 3022, 43], §14, in *Ancient Near Eastern Texts Relating to the Old Testament*, by J. B. Pritchard (Princeton: Princeton University Press, 1955), 19b.

18. See Cicero, *De republica*, ed. K. Ziegler (Leipzig: Teubner, 1960), 6.1.1 (p. 122).

19. See J. Cohen, *"Be Fertile and Increase, Fill the Earth and Master It": The Ancient and Medieval Career of a Biblical Text* (Ithaca, NY: Cornell University Press, 1989).

20. See above, in the section "Modern Times as a Project."

21. Kant, *Kritik der reinen Vernunft*, preface, Bxii–xiv.

22. F. W. J. Schelling, *Einleitung zu dem Entwurf eines Systems der Naturphilosophie*, para. 4, in *Ausgewählte Werke, 1799–1801* (Darmstadt: Wissenschaftliche Buchgesellschaft, 1980), 276.

23. *The Federalist*, ed. J. E. Cooke (Middletown, CT: Wesleyan University Press, 1961), no. 14 (James Madison) (pp. 88–89); See P. Gay, *The Enlightenment: An Interpretation*, vol. 2, *The Science of Freedom* (New York: Norton, 1969), 566.

24. E. Renan, *L'Avenir de la science*, chap. 8, n. 68, in *Oeuvres Complètes*, ed. H. Psichari (Paris: Calmann-Lévy, 1947–), 3:1133.

25. J. S. Mill, *On Liberty*, ch. 3, in *"Utilitarianism," "On Liberty," "Representative Government,"* ed. A. D. Lindsay (London: Dent [Everyman], 1948), 115; see also p. 122 and ch. 4, p. 137.

26. Nietzsche, frag. 6 [48], Summer 1875, in *KSA*, 8:115–18.

27. See R. Shattuck, *The Innocent Eye: On Modern Literature and the Arts* (New York: Washington Square Press, 1986), 78–81.

28. The classical Hebrew commentators all understand the passage as a reminder of the shortness of life, as do the translators of the King James Ver-

sion. The Vulgate (*militia*) and Luther (*im Dienst stehen*) and many modern English versions choose the idea of "service." (Unless otherwise noted—as here—translations from the Bible are from the New Revised Standard Version [NRSV].)

29. Augustine, *Confessions* 10.28.39; in Bibliothèque Augustinienne (hereafter BA), 14:210.

30. Maimonides, *Guide of the Perplexed*, ed. Y. Joel (Jerusalem: Junovitch, 1929), 3.24 (p. 361, line 27, through p. 362, line 5); trans. S. Pines (Chicago: University of Chicago Press, 1962), 498.

31. A. Villiers de l'Isle-Adam, *L'Ève Future*, ed. N. Satiat (Paris: Garnier-Flammarion, 1992), bk. 2, ch. 4, p. 187.

32. Goethe, conversation with Johann Daniel Falk (no. 1185), June 14, 1809, in *Goethes Gespräche: Gesamtausgabe*, ed. F. von Biedermann et al., vol. 2, *Vom Erfurter Kongress bis zum letzten böhmischen Aufenthalt* (Leipzig: Biedermann, 1909), 41, my emphasis; for the context see P. Hadot, *Le Voile d'Isis: Essai sur l'histoire de l'idée de nature* (Paris: Gallimard, 2004), 263.

33. See above, in the section "Modern Times as a Project."

34. J. G. Fichte, *Grundlage des Naturrechts* [1796], II, §6, η, in *Ausgewählte Werke*, ed. F. Medicus (Darmstadt: Wissenschaftliche Buchgesellschaft, 1962), 2:83; M. Heidegger, *Sein und Zeit* (Tubingen: Niemeyer, 1963), §30, p. 142; Heidegger, *Vom Wesen des Grundes* [1929], III, in *Wegmarken* (Frankfurt: Klostermann, 1967), 59–64; "Brief über den 'Humanismus,'" in *Wegmarken*, 169.

35. R. M. Rilke, "Wie die Natur die Wesen überlässt . . . ," in *Gedichte, 1910–1926*, ed. M. Engel and U. Fülleborn, vol. 2 in *Werke, Kommentierte Ausgabe in 4 Bänden* (Frankfurt: Insel, 1996), 324; Heidegger, "Wozu Dichter?," in *Holzwege* (Frankfurt: Klostermann, 1950), 248–95, especially 255ff. The word "risk" is also in Hans Jonas, *Das Prinzip Verantwortung: Versuch einer Ethik für die technologische Zivilisation* (Frankfurt: Insel, 1979), 247 (translated into English by Hans Jonas and David Herr as *The Imperative of Responsibility: In Search of an Ethics for the Technological Age* [Chicago: University of Chicago Press, 1984]).

36. J. Huxley, *What Dare I Think? The Challenge of Modern Science to Human Action and Belief* (London: Chatto & Windus, 1931), ch. 5, pp. 150–51, then 177; see also ch. 5, p. 169.

37. Jonas, *Das Prinzip Verantwortung*, 188; see also 280.

38. Nietzsche, *Also sprach Zarathustra*, prologue, 3, in *KSA*, 4:14.

39. See Abu Hātim al-Rāzi, *The Proofs of Prophecy*, a parallel English-Arabic text translated, introduced, and annotated by T. Khalidi (Provo, UT: Brigham Young University Press, 2011), 9.

40. Alexander von Villers, letter to Warsberg, April 30, 1873; in *Briefe eines Unbekannten*, ed. M. Gideon (Zurich: Manesse, n.d.), 245.

41. Ernst Barlach, quoted in H. Sedlmayr, *Verlust der Mitte: Die bildende Kunst des 19. und 20. Jahrhunderts als Symptom und Symbol der Zeit* (Salzburg: Otto Müller, 1948), 157.

42. F. Dostoyevsky, Дневник писателя [Dnevnik pisatelja; A writer's diary] [1876] October 1876, issue no. 1, article 4, in Собрание сочинений [Sobranie sotchineniyi; Collected works], vol. 13 (Saint Petersburg: Nauka, 1994), 322 (translated into English by K. Lantz as *A Writer's Diary*, 2 vols. [Evanston, IL: Northwestern University Press, 1993–94]). On the impossibility of cursing an experimenter who is supposed to be absent, see also Stephen Crane, "The Open Boat" [1899], in *The Red Badge of Courage, and Other Stories* (London: Penguin, 1983), 246.

43. F. Dostoyevsky, Братья Карамазовы [Brat'ya Karamazovy; *The Brothers Karamazov*] (Moscow: ACT, 2006), pt. 2, bk. 5, ch. 5, p. 265. The sentence looks like a quote (quotation marks!). It might allude to N. Strakhov's critique of the authors according to which man is only a transitory form, an essay of nature doomed to be superseded by a superior being; see D. Čyževskyj, "Literarische Lesefrüchte. IV," *Zeitschrift für Slavische Philologie* 13 (1936): 70. I owe this reference to Professor Birgit Harress (Leipzig).

44. J. D. Bernal, *The World, the Flesh and the Devil: An Inquiry into the Future of the Three Enemies of the Rational Soul* [1929] (London: Jonathan Cape, 1970), ch. 5, p. 64 (last words of the chapter).

45. Nietzsche, *Morgenröte*, III, aphorism 187, in *KSA*, 3:160; V, aphorism 432, in *KSA*, 3:266; aphorism 453, in *KSA*, 3:274; aphorism 501, in *KSA*, 3:294; *Die fröhliche Wissenschaft*, I, aphorism 51, in *KSA*, 3:415–16; III, aphorism 110, in *KSA*, 3:471; IV, aphorism 324, in *KSA*, 3:552; *Jenseits von Gut und Böse*, V, aphorism 203, in *KSA*, 5:126.

46. Nietzsche, frag. 25 [305], Spring 1884, in *KSA*, 11:88. The exclamation *wohlan!* has in Nietzsche almost the value of a concept.

47. P. G. Wodehouse, *Jeeves in the Offing* (London: Penguin Books, 1963), ch. 90, p. 80.

48. L. Tolstoy, Крейцерова соната, ed. and trans. into French by S. Luneau as *La Sonate à Kreutzer* (Paris: Gallimard, 1994), ch. 11, p. 108 (translated into English by J. D. Huff and A. Maude in *"The Kreutzer Sonata," "The Devil," and Other Stories* [London: Oxford University Press, 1973]).

49. D. Benatar, *Better Not to Have Been: The Harm of Coming into Existence* (Oxford: Oxford University Press, 2006).

Chapter Two   Atheism at the End of the Tether

1. Edmund Burke, *Thoughts on French Affairs*, in *Further Reflections on the Revolution in France*, ed. D. E. Ritchie (Indianapolis: Liberty Fund, 1992), 237.

2. Galileo Galilei, *Il saggiatore* [1623], ch. 6, https://it.wikisource.org/wiki/Il_Saggiatore/6 (translated into English by W. R. Shea and M. Davie as *The Assayer* [extracts], in *Galileo: Selected Writings* [Oxford: Oxford University Press, 2012]).

3. Dietrich Bonhoeffer, "Gedanken zum Tauftag von D. W. R." [May 25, 1944], in *Widerstand und Ergebung: Briefe und Aufzeichnungen aus der Haft*, ed. E. Bethge (Gütersloh: Mohn, 1985), 155.

4. See R. Brague, *Moderately Modern* (South Bend, IN: St. Augustine's Press, forthcoming 2019), ch. 4.

5. Pierre Bayle, *Pensées diverses sur la Comète*, ed. A. Prat and P. Rétat (Paris: Champion, 1994), §§113–32, 301–50.

6. See Thomas H. Huxley, *Life and Letters*, ed. L. Huxley (London: Macmillan, 1900), 1:343–44.

7. See, for example, Auguste Comte, *Discours préliminaire sur l'esprit positif*, ch. 1, in *Philosophie des sciences*, ed. J. Grange (Paris: Gallimard, 1996), p. 138; Claude Bernard, *Leçons sur les phénomènes de la vie communs aux animaux et aux végétaux* (Paris: Baillière, 1878), appendix, p. 397.

8. T. W. Adorno and M. Horkheimer, *Dialektik der Aufklärung: Philosophische Fragmente* [1944] (Frankfurt: Fischer, 1969).

9. See R. Brague, *The Wisdom of the World*, trans. T. Fagan (Chicago: University of Chicago Press, 2005); Brague, *The Law of God*, trans. L. Cochrane (Chicago: University of Chicago Press, 2009).

10. Karl Marx, *Zur Kritik der Hegelschen Rechtsphilosophie*, Einleitung, in *Frühe Schriften*, ed. S. Landshut, 7th ed. (Stuttgart: Kröner, 2004), 283.

11. See Jean-Paul Sartre, *L'Existentialisme est un humanisme* (Paris: Nagel, 1946), 91–92.

12. See above, under "The Successes of a Nontheistic Worldview," 24–26.

13. Jean-Jacques Rousseau, *La Profession de foi du vicaire savoyard* (Profession of faith of the Savoyard curate; = *Émile*, pt. 4), in *Oeuvres Complètes* (Paris: Gallimard, 1969), 4:632–33.

14. See A. Schopenhauer, *Die Welt als Wille und Vorstellung*, bk. 4, ch. 44, "Metaphysik der Geschlechterliebe," in *Werke*, ed. E. von Lohneysen (Darmstadt: Wissenschaftliche Buchgesellschaft, 1980), 2:678–727.

15. C. Darwin, *The Descent of Man*, ch. 5, "Natural Selection as Affecting Civilized Nations" (New York: Random House, n.d.), 501–5.

16. See the recent synthesis of A. Gotman, *Pas d'enfant: La volonté de ne pas engendrer* (Paris: Maison des Sciences de l'Homme, 2017).

17. Thomas Aquinas, *Summa theologica* I.2.3.

18. See R. Brague, *On the God of the Christians*, trans. P. Seaton (South Bend, IN: St. Augustine's Press, 2013).

19. See E. E. Evans-Pritchard, *Theories of Primitive Religion* (Oxford: Clarendon Press, 1965), 54.

20. *Aggivaccha Sutta* (N. 72), in *The Teachings of Buddha: A New Translation of the Majjhima Nikāya*, trans. B. Ñāṇamoli (Boston: Wisdom Publications, 1995), 590–94, especially 591–92; Sankara, *Svâtma-nirûpana*, 93, quoted in H. von Glasenapp, *Der Stufenweg zum Göttlichen: Shankaras Philosophie der All-Einheit* (Baden-Baden: Bühler, 1948), 74–75.

21. Mishna *Hagiga*, ch. 2. See R. Brague, "L'Idée de curiosité dans le judaïsme et l'Islam pré-modernes: Pour ouvrir un dossier," in *Torah et Science: Perspectives historiques et théoriques; Études offertes à C. Touati*, ed. G. Freudenthal, J.-P. Rothschild, and G. Dahan (Paris and Leuven: Peeters, 2001), 131–46.

22. Irenaeus, *Adversus haereses*, ed. A. Rousseau et al., Sources chrétiennes 100 (Paris: Cerf, 1968), 4.20.7 (p. 648).

23. H. G. Wells, *Mind at the End of Its Tether* (London and Toronto: W. Heinemann, 1945).

Chapter Three   The Necessity of Goodness

1. See Brague, *Anchors in the Heavens*, ch. 10.

2. Aristotle, *Nicomachean Ethics* 1.7.1097a23.

3. Aristotle, *Metaphysics* Z.8.1033b28; other texts in H. Bonitz, *Index aristotelicus* (Graz: Akademische Verlagsanstalt, 1955 [= 1870]), col. 599a46–49.

4. References in Bonitz, *Index aristotelicus*, col. 59b40–45.

5. Aristotle, *Physics* 2.2.194b13; Cervantes, *Don Quijote*, ed. F. Rico (Madrid: Prisa, 2012), pt. 2, ch. 45, p. 887.

6. Kant, *Von einem neuerdings erhobenen vornehmen Ton in der Philosophie*, in *Werke*, ed. W. Weischedel (Darmstadt: Wissenschaftliche Buchgesellschaft, 1983), 3:382.

7. Aristotle, *Politics* 1.2.1252b29–30.

8. Aristotle, *Nicomachean Ethics* 10.4.1174b33.

9. Aristotle, *On the Soul* 2.8.420b17–22.

10. Aristotle, *Peri philosophias*, §24, in *Fragmenta selecta*, ed. W. D. Ross (Oxford: Oxford University Press, 1955), 92.

11. Aristotle, *On the Soul* 3.13.

12. Phokylides, frag. 9, in *Anthologia lyrica graeca*, ed. E. Diehl (Leipzig: Teubner, 1936), 1:60; Plato, *Republic* 3.407a.

13. Analogous formula in Cicero, quoted by Lactantius, *Divinae institutiones*, ed. E. Heck and A. Wlosok (Berlin and New York: De Gruyter, 2007), 3.14.17 (p. 248); A. Schopenhauer, *Die Welt als Wille und Vorstellung*, bk. 4, ch. 46, in *Werke*, 2:746.

14. Machiavelli, *Storie fiorentine*, bk. 3, pt. 4, para. 13, in *Tutte le opere storiche, politiche e letterarie*, ed. A. Capata (Rome: Newton Compton, 2011), 541. The saying is Machiavelli's invention.

15. B. Brecht, *Die Dreigroschenoper* [1928], act 2, "Wovon lebt der Mensch."

16. Boethius, *Consolation of Philosophy* 1, pr. 12, p. 304; 4, pr. 2, p. 326; 4, pr. 3, p. 334.

17. Ibid., 3, pr. 11, p. 288.

18. See Ps.-Dionysius, *Divine Names* 5.1 (PG 3:816b).

19. Aristotle, *Nicomachean Ethics* 6.2.1139a20.

20. I. Kant, *Kritik der praktischen Vernunft*, pt. 1, bk. 1, ch. 1, §7, ed. K. Vorländer (Hamburg: Meiner, 1929), 37–38.

21. I. Kant, *Kritik der reinen Vernunft*, Elementarlehre, I, "Transzendentale Ästhetik," 2, "Von der Zeit," B72.

22. A. Schopenhauer, *Preisschrift über die Grundlage der Moral*, §6, in *Werke*, 3:658.

23. I. Kant, *Zum ewigen Frieden*, 1, "Zusatz: Von der Garantie des ewigen Friedens," in *Werke*, 6:224.

24. D. Hume, "On the Independency of Parliament" [1741], in *Essays Moral, Political and Literary*, World's Classics (Oxford: Oxford University Press, 1963), 40, 42.

25. Augustine, *City of God*, ed. C. J. Perl (Paderborn: Schöningh, 1979), 19.12 (2:466).

26. J. Maritain, *Trois Réformateurs: Luther, Descartes, Rousseau*, pt. 2, ch. 3, in *Oeuvres Complètes* (Fribourg: Éditions universitaires; Paris: Éditions Saint-Paul, 1984), (3:488).

27. Hegel, *Philosophie der Geschichte*, Einleitung, ed. H. Glockner (Stuttgart: Frommann, 1958), 11:46.

28. Hegel, *Philosophie des Rechts*, §124 (Glockner, 7:182).

29. Augustine, *City of God* 12.6 (Perl, 1:788).

30. Aquinas, *Summa theologica* I.63.5–6, c.

31. Milton, *Paradise Lost*, bk. 5, line 860, and see C. S. Lewis, *A Preface to "Paradise Lost"* (Oxford: Oxford University Press, 1960) 97–98.

32. S. Kierkegaard, *L'Alternative* [1843], pt. 2, French trans. P.-H. Tisseau and E.-M. Jacquet-Tisseau (Paris: L'Orante, 1970), 4:194.

33. C. Darwin, letter to Joseph Hooker, February 1, 1871.

34. H. Arendt, *The Human Condition* [1958] (Chicago: University of Chicago Press, 1998), 9, and elsewhere in Arendt's work.

35. R. M. Rilke, *Das Stunden-Buch*, bk. 3, *Das Buch von der Armut und vom Tode* [1903], in *Werke in drei Bänden*, ed. B. Allemann, vol. 1, *Gedicht-Zyklen* (Frankfurt: Insel, 1966), 103.

36. E. Levinas, *Totalité et infini: Essai sur l'extériorité* (The Hague: Nijhoff, 1961), 199.

37. F. Dostoyevsky, *Notes from the Underground*, pt. 2, ch. 10, trans. C. Garnett (Indianapolis: Hackett, 2009).

38. G. Anders, *Die Antiquiertheit des Menschen*, vol. 1, *Über die Zerstö-rung der Seele im Zeitalter der zweiten industriellen Revolution* (Munich: Beck, 2010), 23–95.

39. Nietzsche, *Also sprach Zarathustra*, pt. 1, prologue, 3, in *KSA*, 4:14.

40. Plato, *Republic* 509b.

41. See n. 4.

42. See Brague, *Wisdom of the World*, 62–70.

43. D. Hume, *Dialogues concerning Natural Religion* [1779], ed. J.C. A. Gaskin (Oxford: Oxford University Press, 1993), ch. 5, pp. 67–69.

44. R. Dawkins, *The Blind Watchmaker* (London: Penguin, 1986).

Chapter Four   Nature

1. I. Kant, *Kritik der Urteilskraft*, ed. K. Vorländer (Hamburg: Meiner, 1924), §59.

2. J. G. Fichte, *Das System der Sittenlehre nach den Prinzipien der Wis-senschaftslehre* [1798], "2. Hauptstück," in *Ausgewählte Werke in sechs Bän-den*, ed. F. Medicus (Darmstadt: Wissenschaftliche Buchgesellschaft, 1962), 2:457–59.

3. See Brague, *Wisdom of the World*, 216.

4. See R. Brague, "Is Physics Interesting? Some Responses from Late An-tiquity and the Middle Ages," in *The Legend of the Middle Ages: Philosophical Explorations of Medieval Christianity, Judaism and Islam*, trans. L. Cochrane (Chicago: University of Chicago Press, 2009), 73–74.

5. F. Bacon, *Novum Organon*, ed. W. Krohn (Darmstadt: Wissenschaft-liche Buchgesellschaft, 1990), bk. 1, para. 48, p. 110; bk. 2, II, p. 280.

6. Kant, *Kritik der Urteilskraft*, §75.

7. See further in ch. 5, under "Freedom as Free Access to the Good."

8. See A. Ferrarin, *Galilei e la matematica della natura* (Pisa: ETS, 2014), 81.

9. E. Voegelin, *The New Science of Politics: An Introduction* (Chicago: University of Chicago Press, 1952), ch. 4, "Gnosticism—The Nature of Moder-nity," 107–32.

10. R. Girard, *Mensonge romantique et vérité romanesque* (Paris: Grasset, 1961), ch. 9, pp. 222–24.

11. Leo Strauss, *Natural Right and History* (Chicago: University of Chi-cago Press, 1953), 81.

12. See J. Klatzkin, *Thesaurus Philosophicus linguae hebraicae et veteris et recentioris* [Hebrew] (New York: Feldheim, 1968), s.v. 'teva (in vol. 2, pp. 9–13).

13. Aristotle, *Metaphysics*, Δ.4.1014b16–17.

14. See Ernest Klein, *A Comprehensive Etymological Dictionary of the Hebrew Language for Readers of English* (New York: Macmillan, 1987), s.v. *ṭevaʿ* (pp. 239–40).

15. See H. Bonitz, *Index aristotelicus* (Graz: Akademische Druck- und Verlagsanstalt, 1955 [= 1870]), col. 59, lines 41–45 (eighteen occurrences).

16. See for example Augustine, *Letter 138*, I, 5 (PL 33:527) (*carmen*), and *Letter 166*, V, 13 (PL 33:726) (*canticus*).

17. See Brague, *Legitimacy of the Human*, 131–33 (end of ch. 7).

18. Bernard of Clairvaux, *De gratia et libero arbitrio* 6.17, in *Opera*, vol. 3, ed. J. Leclercq and H. M. Rochais (Rome: Editiones Cistercienses, 1963), 178–79 (or PL 182:1011ab).

19. Augustine, *De Genesi ad litteram*, ed. J. Zycha, Corpus Scriptorum Ecclesiasticorum Latinorum, tome 28, vol. 1 (Prague: Tempsky, 1894), 4.33 (p. 132).

20. C. Darwin, *The Origin of Species*, ch. 15, "Conclusion" (New York: Modern Library, n.d.), 374.

21. William IX of Aquitaine, "Ab la dolchor . . . ," in *Provenzalische Chrestomathie . . .* , by C. Appel (Leipzig: Reisland, 1930), poem 10, p. 51, col. a (*li aucel / canton, chascus, en lor lati* [the birds sing, each in its own Latin]); Cercamon, "Quant l'aura doussa . . . ," in ibid., poem 13, p. 53, col. a; Chrétien de Troyes, *Perceval*, lines 71–72, in *Oeuvres Complètes*, ed. D. Poirion (Paris: Gallimard, 1994), 687; Jean de Meung, *Roman de la rose*, ed. F. Lecoy (Paris: Champion, 1973), line 8378 (2:6); G. Cavalcanti, "Fresca rosa novella . . . ," lines 10–11, in *Rime*, ed. D. de Robertis (Turin: Einaudi, 1986); Geoffrey Chaucer, The Squire's Tale, line 478 (*haukes ledene*), in *The Canterbury Tales*; O. Mandelstam, "Аббат" [Abbat; Abbot], in *Камень* [*Kamen'*], in *Стихотворения: Проза* [Stikhotvorenija; Proza (Poems; prose)] (Moscow: EKSMO, 2011), 100.

22. Arnaut Daniel, poem 12, beginning, "Doutz braitz e critz . . ."

23. Theodorus of Asine, quoted by Proclus, *Commentary on the Timaeus*, ed. E. Diehl (Leipzig: Teubner, 1903), pt. 2 (1:213).

24. Gregory of Nazianzus, *Hymn 29* (PG 37:508a).

25. Augustine, *De Genesi ad litteram* 9.17, 32–18, 33, in Zycha, pp. 291–92; and see also 6.13, 24, in Zycha, p. 188. See the Arabic extract from Ignatius of Antioch's letters, in *The Apostolic Fathers . . .* , ed. J. B. Lightfoot (London: Macmillan, 1890), 2nd series, vol. 3 (p. 301).

26. See Ibn Hazm, *Al-Fiṣal fī 'l-Milal wa-'l-ahwā' wa-l-nihal* [The separator concerning religions, heresies, and sects], ed. A. Šams ad-Din (Beirut: Dar al-kutub al-ilmiya, 1999), 2.18 (2:84); 2.20 (2:124); the same passage may be found in Spanish translation in M. Asín Palacios, *Abenházam de Córdoba y su historia crítica de las ideas religiosas* (Madrid: Revista de archivos, bibliotecas y museos, 1930), 3:285, 322.

27. Maimonides, *Guide of the Perplexed*, ed. Y. Joel (Jerusalem: Junovitch, 1929), 1.73, 10th proposition (p. 145, line 10, through p. 146, line 10); English trans. in *Guide of the Perplexed*, trans. S. Pines (Chicago: University of Chicago Press 1963), 207–9.

28. N. Malebranche, *De La Recherche de la vérité*, XVᵉ Eclaircissement, 5ᵉ preuve, in *Oeuvres*, ed. G. Rodis-Lewis (Paris: Gallimard, 1979), 1:987–88.

29. Aquinas, *Summa contra gentiles* III.69 (Rome: Leonina, 1934), 303b.

30. P. Duhem, *Le Système du monde: Histoire des doctrines cosmologiques de Platon à Copernic* (Paris: Hermann, 1913–59).

31. Alan of Lille, *De planctu naturae*, ed. W. Wetherbee (Cambridge, MA: Harvard University Press, 2013), ch. 6, §3 (p. 68), §9 (p. 74); ch. 8, §30 (p. 108 [*pro-dea*]); ch. 16, §25 (p. 194); ch. 18, §4 (p. 204); Jean de Meung, *Le Roman de la rose*, ed. F. Lecoy (Paris: Champion, 1973), line 16752 (3:3), and line 19477 (3:85); Geoffrey Chaucer, The Physician's Tale, line 20, in *Canterbury Tales*.

32. See Brague, *Legend of the Middle Ages*, 85–87.

33. Aquinas, *Summa contra gentiles* II.2, 3. See Brague, *Wisdom of the World*, 174–75.

34. Aquinas, *Summa contra gentiles* II.3, p. 95a. See ibid. III.120, p. 372b.

Chapter Five   Freedom and Creation

1. See R. Brague, "God and Freedom: Biblical Roots of the Western Idea of Liberty," in *Christianity and Freedom*, ed. T. S. Shah and A. D. Hertzke, vol. 1, *Historical Perspectives* (Cambridge: Cambridge University Press, 2016), 391–402.

2. Rousseau, *Le Contrat social*, bk. 1, ch. 7, in *Oeuvres Complètes* (Paris: Gallimard, 1964), 3:364.

3. See J. L. Talmon, *The Origins of Totalitarian Democracy* (London: Secker & Warburg, 1952, 1960).

4. B. de Spinoza, letter 58, in *Opera*, ed. J. Van Vloten and J. P. N. Land (The Hague: Nijhoff, 1914), 3:196.

5. Kant, *Kritik der praktischen Vernunft*, pt. 1, bk. 1, ch. 3, "Kritische Beleuchtung . . . " (p. 109).

6. Alexander of Aphrodisias, *De anima liber*, ed. I. Bruns (Berlin: Reimer, 1887), p. 175, lines 8–9; Gregory of Nyssa, *Catechetical Discourse* 5.9–10 (PG 45:24c); Bernard of Clairvaux, *De gratia et libero arbitrio* 9.28–29, in *Opera*, 3:185 (or PL 182:1016b–c); *Sermon on the Annunciation* 1.7, in *Opera*, 5:19 (or PL 183:386c); Pierre de Jean Olieu, *Quaestiones in II. Sententiarum* [Questions on the second part of Peter Lombard's *Book of Sentences*], ed. B. Jansen (Florence: Quaracchi, 1924), q. 57 (2:338).

7. Rousseau, *Discours sur l'origine de l'inégalité*, pt. 1, in *Oeuvres Complètes*, 3:141.

8. Aristotle, *Metaphysics* Θ.2.1046b21.

9. Spinoza, *Tractatus theologico-politicus*, ch. 20, in *Opera*, 2:306; Hume, "On the Origin of Government," in *Essays Moral, Political and Literary*, 39; Lord Acton, "The History of Freedom in Antiquity" [1877], in *Selected Writings of Lord Acton*, ed. J. Rufus Fears, vol. 1, *Essays in the History of Liberty* (Indianapolis: Liberty Fund, 1985), 29.

10. See R. Brague, "God and Freedom: Biblical Roots of the Western Idea of Liberty," in *Christianity and Freedom*, ed. T. S. Shah and A. D. Hertzke, vol. 1, *Historical Perspectives* (Cambridge: Cambridge University Press, 2016), 391–402.

12. W. F. Albright, *From the Stone Age to Christianity: Monotheism and the Historical Process* (New York: Doubleday Anchor Books, 1957), 285.

13. Augustine, *City of God* 12.21 (Perl, 1:832); Arendt, *Human Condition*, 177; Arendt, *The Origins of Totalitarianism* (New York: Schocken, 2004), 616.

14. See for example C. L. Griswold, *Forgiveness: A Philosophical Exploration* (Cambridge: Cambridge University Press, 2007).

15. See N. Murphy and G. F. R. Ellis, *On the Moral Nature of the Universe: Theology, Cosmology, and Ethics* (Minneapolis: Fortress Press, 1996).

16. H. Bergson, *L'Évolution créatrice* [1907] (Paris: Presses Universitaires de France, 1959), ch. 3, p. 249.

17. Augustine, *Confessions* 8, chs. 9–10 (paras. 21–22).

18. Ovid, *Metamorphoses* 7.20–21; Seneca, *Letters to Lucilius*, ed. L. R. Reynolds (Oxford: Oxford University Press, 1965), 21.1 (1:56); Epictetus, *Diatribai*, ed. H. Schenkl (Leipzig: Teubner, 1898), 2.26.4 (p. 203); *Book of Secrets* (1Q27, 8–12), in *The Dead Sea Scrolls Study Edition*, ed. F. García Martinez and E. J. C. Tigchelaar (Leyden: Brill, 1967), 66–68.

19. See S. Pines, "On the Avatars of the Term 'Freedom'" [Hebrew], in *Iyyūn* 33, no. 1–2 (1984): 247–65; my French translation in *La Liberté de philosopher: De Maïmonide à Spinoza* (Paris: Desclée De Brouwer,), 47–86.

20. See for example the statement of Ğuwaynī, al-Ghazali's teacher, in *al-Iršād* [The guide], ed. J. Luciani (Paris: Imprimerie nationale, 1938), ch. 19, para. 20 (p. 145).

21. See R. Brague, "God and Freedom: Biblical Roots of the Western Idea of Liberty," 391–402.

22. Augustine, *Confessions* 13.9.10, in BA, 14:440; see also *City of God* 9.28, in BA, 1:762; *Letter 54*, 10.18 (PL 33:212–13); *Letter 157*, 2.9 (PL 33:677).

23. Aristotle, *On the Heavens* 4.3.311a4; Aristotle, *Physics* 8.5.257b7–8; see also *Metaphysics* Θ.8.1050a7.

24. Bergson, *Essai sur les données immédiates de la conscience* (Paris: Alcan, 1889), ch. 3, p. 129.

25. Hesiod, *Works and Days* 287–92; Prodikos in Xenophon, *Memorabilia* 2.1.21–33; Robert Frost, "The Road Not Taken" [1916], in *The Poetry of Robert Frost*, ed. Edward Connery Lathem (New York: Holt, Rinehart and Winston, 1969), 105.

26. See for example Jean de Meung, *Roman de la rose*, lines 21533–34 (Lecoy, 3:147).

27. Dante, "Purgatorio," canto 10, lines 124–26, in *La divina commedia*. The translation is from Charles Singleton's translation (Princeton: Princeton University Press, 1970–75).

Chapter Six   Culture as a By-Product

1. Benedikt XVI, "Wurzeln der europäischen Kultur: Begegnung mit Vertretern aus der Welt der Kultur," speech delivered in Paris, September 12, 2008, published in *Die Ökologie des Menschen: Die großen Reden des Papstes* (Munich: Pattloch, 2012), 330–41.

2. Aristotle, *Metaphysics* A.1.981b17–25.

3. Horace, *Sermones* 1.8.1–3. See also the parable enacted by the upstart Amasis in Herodotus 2.172.

4. Kant, *Kritik der Urteilskraft*, §2 (p. 41 and footnote).

5. C. S. Lewis, "Our English Syllabus" [1939], in *Image and Imagination: Essays and Reviews*, ed. W. Hooper (Cambridge: Cambridge University Press, 2013), 23.

6. See H. de Lumley, "Quand la culture apparaît-elle?," in *Culture et transcendance: Chemins de la création culturelle*, ed. D. Ponnau, M. Morange, and J. Duchesne (Paris: Parole et Silence, 2015), 119.

7. Benedikt XVI, "Wurzeln der europäischen Kultur, 331.

8. See the recent synthesis of F. Cardini, *Cassiodoro il grande: Roma, i barbari e il monachesimo* (Milan: Jaca Book, 2009), especially ch. 3, para. 3, pp. 139–49.

9. Cassiodorus, *Institutiones* 1.1 (PL 70:1005).

10. E. Gibbon, *Autobiography*, ed. J. B. Bury (London: Oxford University Press, 1907), 160.

11. See R. Brague, "Jew, Greek and Christian: Some Reflections on the Pauline Revolution," in *Expositions: Interdisciplinary Studies in the Humanities* 1, no. 1 (March 2007): 15–28.

12. See R. Brague, "Inclusion and Digestion: Two Models of Cultural Appropriation," in *Legend of the Middle Ages*, 145–58.

13. See for example Ibn Qayyim al-Jawziyya, *Medicine of the Prophet*, trans. P. Johnstone (Cambridge: Islamic Texts Society, 1998).

14. *To Diognetus*, ed. H.-I. Marrou, 2nd ed., Sources chrétiennes 33, 2nd expanded ed. (Paris: Cerf, 1965), 62.

15. Pascal, *Lettres Provinciales*, no. 14, in *Oeuvres Complètes*, ed. L. Lafuma (Paris: Seuil, 1963), 435a.

16. Benedikt XVI, "Wurzeln der europäischen Kultur," 337–38.

17. C. S. Lewis, *Reflections on the Psalms* [1961] (Glasgow: Collins, 1977), ch. 9, pp. 77–83, quotation from 82.

18. Hermogenes of Tarsos, *Peri ideon* 2.10, "Peri logou politikou," in *Hermogenis Opera*, ed. H. Rabe (Leipzig: Teubner, 1913), 389, quoted in E. R. Curtius, *Europäische Literatur und lateinisches Mittelalter*, 8th ed. (Bern and Munich: Francke, 1973), 164.

19. H. Friedrich, *Die Struktur der modernen Lyrik: Von der Mitte des neunzehnten bis zur Mitte des zwanzigsten Jahrhunderts* (Berlin: Rowohlt, 1967), 30. My trans.

20. Nietzsche, *Morgenröte*, V, aphorism 456, in *KSA*, 3:275.

21. M. Barrès, *Le Culte du Moi: "Sous l'œil des barbares," "Un Homme libre," "Le Jardin de Bérénice"* [1888–91] (Paris: Plon, 1966).

22. Benedikt XVI, "Wurzeln der europäischen Kultur," 334.

23. Montaigne, *Essais*, ed. J. Céard et al. (Paris: La Pochothèque, 2001), bk. 2, essay 9 (p. 1477).

24. Benedikt XVI, "Wurzeln der europäischen Kultur," 333–34.

25. Ps.-Bernard, *De cantu* 7 (PL 182:1128a). On the origin of the phrase, see Plato, *Statesman*, 273d, and Augustine, *Confessions* 7.10.16.

26. Benedikt XVI, "Wurzeln der europäischen Kultur," 334.

27. John Paul II, *Evangelium Vitae* [encyclical] (March 25, 1995), §12.

Chapter Seven   Values or Virtues?

1. M. Scheler, *Der Formalismus in der Ethik und die materiale Wertethik: Neuer Versuch der Grundlegung eines ethischen Personalismus* [1913], ed. C. Bermes (Hamburg: Meiner, 2014); Scheler, *Das Ressentiment im Aufbau der Moralen* [1913], ed. M. S. Frings (Frankfurt: Klostermann, 1978); see further Heidegger, *Einleitung in die Phänomenologie der Religion* (winter semester 1920–21), in *Phänomenologie des religiösen Lebens* (Frankfurt: Klostermann, 1995), in Heidegger, *Gesamtausgabe* (hereafter *GA*) (Frankfurt: Klostermann, 1975–), 60:120.

2. P. G. Wodehouse, *The Code of the Woosters* [1938] (London: Penguin, n.d.), ch. 5, p. 102.

3. Plato, *Republic* 1.335b8.

4. Molière, *Le malade imaginaire* [1673], 3rd interlude.

5. See Brague, *On the God of the Christians*, 124, and here, ch. 4, under "Nature in the Bible," 51–53.

6. See P. Manent, *La Cité de l'homme* (Paris: Fayard, 1994), 41, 50, 71, 288.

7. Fichte, *Grundlage der gesamten Wissenschaftslehre* [1794], ed. F. Medicus (Darmstadt: Wissenschaftliche Buchgesellschaft, 1962), pt. 3, §5, ch. 2 (1:454).

8. G. E. R. Moore, *Principia ethica* [1903], ed. T. Baldwin (Cambridge: Cambridge University Press, 1993).

9. See above, under "The Virtue of Virtues," 84–86.

10. Nietzsche, *Jenseits von Gut und Böse*, I, aphorism 3, in *KSA*, 5:17; frag. 7 [38], Fall 1887, in *KSA*, 12:352; frag. 11 [73], November 1887–March 1888, in *KSA*, 12:36.

11. Sancti Ambrosii Mediolani, *De officiis ministrorum*, ed. M. Testard, Corpus Christianorum: Series Latina 15 (Turnhout: Brepols, 2000).

12. Thomas Aquinas, *Summa theologica*, I-II.47–170; Roger Bacon, *Moralis philosophia*, ed. E. Massa (Zurich: Thesaurus mundi, 1953).

13. Miskawayh, *Tahḏīb al-aḫlāq wa-taṭhir al-aʿrāq* [Refinement of morals and cleansing of ethics], ed. H. Tamīr (Beirut: Manšūrāt Dār Maktabat al-Ḥayāt, 1398 hegira = 1977 CE); Yahyā Ibn ʿAdī, *Traité d'éthique*, ed. and trans. M.-T. Urvoy (Paris: Cariscript, 1991); Naṣīr ad-Dīn Ṭūsī, *The Nasirean Ethics*, trans. from the Persian by G. M. Wickens (London: Allen & Unwin, 1964).

14. Al-Ghazali, *Mīzān al ʿAmal* [Scales of action], ed. S. Dunya (Cairo: Dār al-Maʿārif, n.d.), chs. 16–19, pp. 264–87.

15. Maimonides, *Eight Chapters*, in *Ethical Writings of Maimonides*, ed. R. L. Weiss and C. Butterworth (New York: New York University Press, 1975), 59–95. See R. L. Weiss, *Maimonides' Ethics: The Encounter of Philosophic and Religious Morality* (Chicago: University of Chicago Press, 1991).

16. Pindar, Pythian ode 2, line 72/131; Nietzsche, *Ecce Homo*, subtitle: *Wie man wird, was man ist* [How one becomes what one is].

17. See Brague, *Legitimacy of the Human*, ch. 9, especially under "Refractions of the 'Be!'"

Chapter Eight   The Family

1. Plato, *Republic* 5.457cd.

2. F. Furet and R. Halévi, *La Monarchie républicaine: La Constitution de 1791* (Paris: Fayard, 1996), Annexe 21, p. 465.

3. H. Taine, "La Révolution," pt. 2, ch. 3, para. 6, in *Les Origines de la France contemporaine* (Paris: Robert Laffont, 1986) 1:464.

4. Alexis de Tocqueville, *Democracy in America*, trans. and ed. Harvey C. Mansfield and Delba Winthrop (Chicago: University of Chicago Press, 2000), 482–84.

5. Beaumarchais, *Le Mariage de Figaro* [1778], 5.3.

6. H. Heine, *Ludwig Börne: Eine Denkschrift* [1837], in *Ein deutsches Zerwürfnis*, ed. H. M. Enzensberger (Nördlingen: Greno, 1986), 139–40.

7. J. B. S. Haldane, *Daedalus, or Science and the Future: A Paper Read to The Heretics, Cambridge on February 4th, 1923* (London: Kegan Paul, Trench, Trubner, 1924), 63–68.

8. Kant, *Kritik der praktischen Vernunft*, pt. 1, bk. 2, ch. 2, para. 5 (p. 149).

9. See Brague, *Anchors in the Heavens*, ch. 5.

10. Aristotle, *Politics* 1.10.1258a21–23.

11. See above, under "The Family under Fire."

12. E. Burke, *Reflections on the Revolution in France* [1790], ed. J. G. A. Pocock (Indianapolis: Hackett, 1987), 29; Tocqueville, *Democracy in America*, 483.

13. John M. Keynes, *A Tract on Monetary Reform* (London: Macmillan, 1924), ch. 3, p. 80.

14. Burke, *Reflections on the Revolution in France*, 83.

Chapter Nine Civilization as Conservation and Conversation

1. Johan Huizinga, *In de schaduwen van morgen: Een diagnose van het geestelijk lijden van onzen tijd* (Haarlem: H. D. Tjeenk Willink & zoon, 1935), ch. 20, p. 202.

2. See Ernest Renan, *De L'origine du langage*, ch. 8, in *Oeuvres Complètes*, ed. H. Psichari (Paris: Calmann-Lévy, 1958), 8:90–91.

3. Ovid, *Tristia* 5.10.37.

4. Andrea A. Robiglio, "Between Language and Likemindedness: Some Aspects of the Concept of Conversatio Civilis from Aquinas to Guazzo," in *Language and Cultural Change: Aspects of the Study and Use of Language in the Later Middle Ages and in the Renaissance*, ed. Lodi Nauta (Leuven: Peeters, 2004), 113–31 [*non vidi*].

5. Roger Scruton, *How to Be a Conservative* (London: Bloomsbury, 2014), 125–32.

6. Marc Fumaroli, *La République des lettres* (Paris: Gallimard, 2015).

7. Thomas Aquinas, *De unitate intellectus contra Averroistas* IV.240, in *Opuscula philosophica*, ed. R. Spiazzi (Turin: Marietti, 1954), 83a. See R. Brague, *Modérément moderne* (Paris: Flammarion, 2014), 200–201.

8. Ibn Khaldun, *Muqaddima*, ed. E. Quatremère (Paris: Didot, 1858), 5.16 (2:307, line 10); F. Rosenthal, at 2:347, translates: "The city . . . is organized."

9. *Stoicorum veterum fragmenta*, ed. H. von Arnim (Leipzig: Teubner, 1903–5; repr., Munich: K. G. Saur, 2004; citation is to 1903–5 ed.), vol. 3, frag. 333–39, pp. 81–83.

10. *The Oxford English Dictionary*, 2nd ed. (Oxford: Clarendon Press, 1989), 3:869a. The most recent example is in Hawthorne (1858).

11. Concerning Adorno and Horkheimer, *Dialektik der Aufklärung*, see above, ch. 2, n. 8; for "barbarism of reflection," Giambattista Vico, *Scienza nuova*, conclusion, §1106, in *Opere*, ed. A. Battistini (Milan: Mondadori, 1990), 1:967; see Stephen T. Holmes, "The Barbarism of Reflection," in *Vico: Past and Present*, ed. G. Tagliacozzo (Atlantic Highlands, NJ: Humanities Press, 1981), 213–22 [*non vidi*].

12. Giacomo Leopardi, *Zibaldone*, ed. L. Felici (Rome: Newton Compton, 2007), 3799–3801, 744b–745b, then 1173, 272b; 1183, 274b.

13. Ibid., 866–867, 202a.

14. Ibid., 21–22 [around 1818], 20b.

15. Ibid., 356, 112b.

16. Ibid., 403, 123a; 868, 202a; 2333, 476b; 1077, 250b.

17. Ibid., 421, 126b.

18. Ibid., 21–22, 20b; see also Juan Donoso Cortés, *Ensayo sobre el catolicismo, el liberalismo y el socialismo* [1851], bk. 1, ch. 1, in *Obras Completas*, ed. J. Juretschke (Madrid: Biblioteca de autores cristianos, 1946), 2:349.

19. J. G. Herder, *Auch eine Philosophie der Geschichte zur Bildung der Menschheit*, 2nd part, "Beginning," in *Werke*, ed. W. Pross (Darmstadt: Wissenschaftliche Buchgesellschaft, 1984), 1:622; see R. Brague, "Völkerwanderungen und Überschwemmungen: Die Flut als Metapher des Vergessens," in *Sintflut und Gedächtnis: Erinnern und Vergessen des Ursprungs*, ed. M. Mulsow and J. Assmann (Munich: Fink, 2006), 117–27.

20. Martin Heidegger, *Überlegungen* (Schwarze Hefte), notebook X, §31 (Frankfurt: Klostermann, 2014), in *GA*, 95:294; notebook XI, §29, in *GA*, 95:386.

21. Ibid., notebook VI, §166, in *GA*, 94:515; see also X, §9, in *GA*, 95:280; XIV, in *GA*, 96:201, 225.

22. Ibid., notebook XIV, in *GA*, 96:229.

23. Ibid., notebook III, §206, in *GA*, 94:194; see also V, §35, in *GA*, 94:330; §147, in *GA*, 94:402.

24. See Karl-Ferdinand Werner, *Naissance de la Noblesse* (Paris: Fayard, 1998).

25. See Caesar, *De bello Gallico*, ed. L. A. Constans (Paris: Belles Lettres, 1926), 6.16 (2:188); Plutarch, *On Superstition*, f. 123; Strabo, *Geography* 4.4.5.

26. See A. Momigliano, *Alien Wisdom: The Limits of Hellenization* (Cambridge: Cambridge University Press, 1975).

27. Lucretius, *De rerum natura* 5.926.

28. Edmund Burke, *Reflections on the Revolution in France*, in *Select Works*, ed. E. J. Payne (Indianapolis: Liberty Fund, 1999), 191, 193.

29. J. Ortega y Gasset, *La rebelión de las masas*, "Prólogo para franceses" [1937], 2nd ed. (Madrid: Tecnos, 2008), ch. 4 (p. 114).

30. John Stuart Mill, *La Liberté*, trans. Charles Dupont-White (Paris: Guillaumin, 1860); Charles Dupont-White, preface, in Mill, *La Liberté*, xxvii; Dupont-White, preface, in Mill, *La Liberté*, 2nd ed. (1864), 27. Auguste Comte sees in continuity a basic condition of scientific and social progress. See his *Cours de Philosophie Positive*, written around 1840, ed. M. Bourdeau (Paris: Hermann, 2012); e.g., lesson 47 (p. 119); 48 (p. 172); 49 (p. 225); 50 (p. 259); 51 (pp. 285, 292, 310n., 317).

31. F. Nietzsche, *Unzeitgemäße Betrachtungen*, essay no. 2, "Über Nutzen und Nachteil der Historie für das Leben," in *KSA*, 1:245–334.

32. J.-P. Sartre, *L'Être et le Néant* [1943] (Paris: Gallimard, 1968), 508.

33. Ossip E. Mandelstam, Буря и натиск [Burya I natisk; Tempest and pression (Russian equivalent of German *Sturm und Drang*)] [1922–23], in Стнхотворения: Проза [Stikhotvorenija-Proza; Poetry-Prose] (Moscow: EKSMO, 2011), 675–76; then Слово и культура [1921] [Slovo i kultura; Word and culture], in ibid., 504; finally, Путешествие в Арменю, Алагез [Pute-šestvie b Armeniu; Trip to Armenia], in ibid., 449.

34. H. Putnam, *Realism with a Human Face* (Cambridge, MA: Harvard University Press, 1990), 135.

35. See Brague, *Wisdom of the World*.

36. Galileo, *Il saggiatore*, ch. 6.

37. See Michel Henry, *La Barbarie* (Paris: Grasset, 1987).

38. The word "culture" derives from the Latin verb *colere*, "to till, culti-vate." See Cicero, *Tusculanae disputationes*, ed. M. Pohlenz (Leipzig: Teubner, 1918), 2.5.13 (p. 286).

39. Augustine, *De Genesi ad litteram* 8.8 (Zycha, p. 243), trans. mine.

40. Lactantius, *De ira Dei*, ed. L. Gasparri (Milan: Bompiani, 2011), 7.5 (p. 52).

41. See H. Blumenberg, *Die Lesbarkeit der Welt* (Frankfurt: Suhrkamp, 1983).

42. See ch. 4, under "The Medieval Outlook Helpful," 53–55.

43. Maimonides, *Guide of the Perplexed*, ed. Y. Joel (Jerusalem: Junovitch, 1929), 1.73, 10th proposition (pp. 144–48; in Pines trans., pp. 206–12).

44. Claude Bernard, *Introduction à l'étude de la médecine expérimentale*, ed. F. Dagognet (Paris: Garnier-Flammarion, 1966), bk. 1, §2, ch. 6 (p. 85).

INDEX

Conrad, Joseph
  The End of the Tether, 34
conservatism, and civilization. *See
    under* civilization
consumerism/materialism, critiques
    of, 22
conversatio civilis, civilization as,
    103–5
cosmogony, 48
cosmography, 48
cosmology, human need for, 47–49
Crane, Stephen
  "The Open Boat," 120n42
creation
  ability of human beings to under-
    stand material universe and, 3
  civilization and, 113–14
  culture and, 81
  freedom and, 63, 64–65
  goodness and, 44–45
  medieval experience of nature as,
    53
  nature and, 52–53, 55–56
cultura animi, 112
culture, 7, 71–82
  aesthetic sense and, 73–74
  barbarism and, 106
  of being, 81–82
  as by-product, 73, 74, 82
  Christianity and, 74, 76–79
  civilization and, 101
  creation and, 81
  of death, 82
  defined, 71–73
  ego/self-expression, reduction to,
    80–81
  etymology of, 133n38
  European, 83
  the family and, 93
  monastic life in the Middle Ages
    and, 74–77, 79
  music and song, 81

as praise, 79–81, 82
religion and, 76–77

Dante, 69–70
Darwin, Charles, 25, 30, 42, 87
  The Origin of Species, 17
Darwinism, 110–11
Dawkins, Richard, 45
death, culture of, 82
Decalogue/Ten Commandments, 76,
    79
deep ecologists, 51, 113
Defoe, Daniel
  An Essay upon Projects, 10
Delors, Jacques, 83
democracy, 50, 59, 91–92, 97–98
Descartes, René, 40
  Discourse on Method, 10
Deuteronomy 30:19, 64, 89
dialectics
  of atheism, 27–28
  of civilization, 105
  of experimentation, 18–19
Dionysius the Areopagite (Pseudo-
    Dionysius), 38
Dostoyevsky, Fyodor
  The Brothers Karamazov, 19
  Diary of a Writer, 19
  Notes from the Underground, 43
Duhem, Pierre, 56
Dupont-White, Charles, 108
Dupré, Louis, 10

Eddington, Arthur, 48
Edison, Thomas, 17
Enlightenment, 9–10, 23, 27, 29–31,
    105
entelechy, 69
environmental destruction and con-
    servation, 21, 28, 51, 99–100,
    113
epainetic genre, 79–80

modern world (*cont.*)
 failure of modern project, 6–7, 9,
  19–21, 22
 the family in, 8, 90–100 (*see also*
  family, the)
 freedom and, 7, 58–70 (*see also*
  freedom)
 goodness in, 7, 35–45 (*see also*
  goodness and the Good)
 madness of, 1–8
 nature and, 7, 46–57 (*see also*
  nature)
 "new Middle Ages," need for,
  4–6
 parasitic, on medieval/Catholic
  values and ideas, 2–4
 project, modernity viewed as, 4,
  6–7, 9–22 (*see also* project,
  modernity viewed as)
 values vs. virtues in, 7–8, 83–89
  (*see also* values vs. virtues)
Molière, 85
monastic life in Middle Ages, 74–77,
 79
Mongols, 107
Montaigne, Michel de, 84
 Essais, 10, 81
Moore, G. E. R., 86–87
morals and morality. *See* values vs.
 virtues
Moses, 79
Moses ben Maimon. *See* Maimonides
Muhammad ibn Zakariyya al-Rāzi,
 18
music and song, 81

Napoleon, 25
natural law, 79
natural reason, knowledge of God
 via, 33
naturalistic fallacy, 87

nature, 7, 46–57
 as barbaric, 110–11
 in the Bible, 51–53, 85–86
 as civilized, 111–13
 cosmology, human sense of,
  47–49
 as creation, 52–53, 55–56
 defined, 46
 as dialogue partner, 113–14
 experimentation and impersonal
  conception of, 16–17
 medieval view of, 53–56, 113
 need for philosophy of, 46–47
 study of, 56–57
 Thomas Aquinas on, 53–54,
  55–56
 understanding of, 49–51
 virtue and, 85–86
Nazism, 101–2, 106
Neoplatonism, 54
Newton, Isaac, 12, 46–47
Nietzsche, Friedrich, 10, 16, 18, 20,
 24, 43, 80, 84, 87, 89, 109
 Thus Spake Zarathustra, 18, 20, 43
Nisibis, convent of, 75
Noah, 79

Oresme, Nicole, 56
Ortega y Gasset, José
 La rebelión de las masas, 108
Ovid, 66, 75, 102–3

pagan culture, 76
paideia, 76
Pascal, Blaise, 79, 84
Paul and Pauline corpus, 14–15, 33,
  75, 76. *See also specific Epistles*
Péguy, Charles, 2
Philippians 3:13, 15
Philosophes, eighteenth-century, 51,
  113
Phokylides, 37

Rémi Brague is emeritus professor of medieval and Arabic philosophy at the University of Paris I and Romano Guardini Chair Emeritus of Philosophy at Ludwig-Maximilians-Universität (Munich). He is the author of a number of books, including *The Kingdom of Man: Genesis and Failure of the Modern Project* (University of Notre Dame Press, 2018).

CPSIA information can be obtained
at www.ICGtesting.com
Printed in the USA
LVHW022007070619
620539LV00008B/105/P